"Readers engaged in or curi⟨...⟩ ⟨...⟩y
to ponder in this eclectic and enlightening collection."
— *Publishers Weekly*

"Every short chapter is a real gem of storytelling, and the characters are unforgettable. This is the one book to give your friends or family members who challenge you with 'Explain this polyamory thing to me, will you?'"
— Kathy Labriola, author of *Love in Abundance* and *The Jealousy Workbook*

"*Stories From the Polycule* gives a good sense of the diversity of polyamory: both the range of ways of doing openly non-monogamous relationships that people have developed, and the numerous different reasons that people have for pursuing them."
— Dr. Meg John Barker, author of *Rewriting the Rules*

"Whether you are new to a poly relationship or have a long-term established poly family, it is affirming to find stories that you relate to. You feel less alone in the world. And for people who don't know a poly family personally, the stories give a human face to the word 'polyamory.'"
— *Red Thread Farm*

PRAISE FOR
THE POLYAMORISTS NEXT DOOR:
INSIDE MULTIPLE-PARTNER RELATIONSHIPS
AND FAMILIES
By Dr. Elisabeth Sheff, 2013

"Elisabeth Sheff has dared to go where few researchers and sociologists have gone before: into the diverse private lives of polyamorous families. This book is a rich resource packed with fascinating portraits of people living, loving, and learning in nontraditional relationships."

> — Tristan Taormino, author of *Opening Up: A Guide to Creating and Sustaining Open Relationships*

"*The Polyamorists Next Door* is an amazingly comprehensive book that is easy to read and relate to. Poly or Mono, you'll find successful ways to navigate relationships interspersed in this fascinating read. I particularly loved Elisabeth Sheff's personal story for its unabashed frankness."

> — Allena Gabosch, Executive Director of the Center and Foundation for Sex Positive Culture and poly activist, educator and coach

"Sheff's new book is a must read for anyone with a curiosity about folks who are able to love more than one person at the same time."

> — Winston Wilde, DHS, LMFT, doctor of human sexuality, licensed marriage & family therapist, certified sex therapist

"We should all be so lucky as to live next door to polyamorists. Their flexibility and willingness to explore alternatives offer clues as to how all families might become more resilient. Dr. Elisabeth Sheff has made a valuable contribution to our understanding of family life."

> — Ann Schranz, Unitarian Universalists for Polyamory Awareness

"There's relatively little written about polyamorists, much less filled with real-world experience, making this a top pick for any collection strong in relationships."

> — *Midwest Book Review*

Stories From the Polycule

ALSO FROM DR. ELISABETH SHEFF

When Someone You Love is Polyamorous
A Guidebook for Family and Friends
Thorntree Press, 2016

The Polyamorists Next Door
Inside Multiple-Partner Relationships and Families
Rowman & Littlefield, 2013

Stories From the Polycule

Real Life in Polyamorous Families

Edited by
Elisabeth Sheff, PhD, CSE, CASA

Thorntree  Press

Thorntree Press, LLC
PO Box 301231
Portland, OR 97294
press@thorntreepress.com

Cover illustration by Tikva Wolf,
creator of Kimchi Cuddles
Cover and interior design by Val Heimpel
Copy-editing by Roma Ilnyckyj
Proofreading by Amy Haagsma

Publisher's Cataloging-In-Publication Data
(Prepared by The Donohue Group, Inc.)

Stories from the polycule : real life in polyamorous families / edited by
  Dr. Elisabeth Sheff.

    pages : illustrations ; cm

    Issued also as an ebook.
    ISBN: 978-0-9913997-7-2

    1. Non-monogamous relationships--Literary collections. 2.
Non-monogamous relationships--Anecdotes. 3. Families--Literary collec-
tions. 4. Families--Anecdotes. 5. Anecdotes. I. Sheff, Elisabeth, 1969-

HQ980 .S76 2015
306.84/23

10 9 8 7 6 5 4 3 2

Printed in the United States of America on acid-free and chlorine-free paper that is made from 100% post-consumer fiber and certified by the Forest Stewardship Council.

Contents

Preface

This is a collection of stories written by people who are, have been, or could possibly be in polyamorous families. Contributors range in age from five years old to sixty-five years old. Some stories are brimming with optimism, others filled with despair. All of them come from the heart.

Stories from the Polycule is composed of six sections. Part 1, "In the beginning," is a collection of stories about how people intentionally start or accidentally end up in poly relationships, when poly folks try to figure out how to be together and ride the exciting feelings at the beginning of relationships. In part 2, "This is what a poly family looks like," contributors explore the range of emotions and complexities, and mundanities, that come with daily life in poly families. "At the kids' table," part 3, presents stories by and about children and parents, and about growing up in a poly family. Part 4, "Things fall apart," explores the difficulties and endings that can come with poly relationships. "For the long haul," part 5, explains how some families stay together, even when they are far apart. The book closes with part 6, "Racy bits," a light-hearted peek at the erotic side of adult poly family life.

I hope you enjoy reading the anthology as much as I have relished putting it together. Thank you to all of the wonderful contributors who made this book possible, the fabulous team at Thorntree Press, and my excellent family, who have supported me while I have brought this project to fruition.

Part I: In the beginning

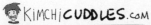

Five lessons on the learning curve
Zac

Q: What happens if you fall in love with someone who's polyamorous, when you aren't even aware it is an 'option'?
A: You learn.

I don't even know if this is unusual in the poly community, as I only experience it via my poly partner. About a year ago, I fell completely head over heels in love with a poly woman.

Who was seeing one of my best friends.

He, and his wife, had recently started seeing her, and I only found out about their relationship a piece at a time. Having known them both for twenty years, I was a little surprised that they never mentioned it to me. It was my future love who did that. I was only a little surprised, and then only at their coyness about it. I had rather hoped that this was the sort of thing they could have mentioned to me without shame. I am, and always have been, comfortable with anyone's sexuality or gender decisions. However, I had never (knowingly!) been around someone who was polyamorous.

From the first moment we met, M and I seemed to *need* to flirt with each other, there were long lingering looks, lots of laughter and me trying very hard to be comforting, funny and impressive, though I certainly didn't think this fabulous, free person would be interested in me, let alone make room in what seemed to be a very busy life, as she talked happily about other 'partners'.

My long-atrophied radar never picked up that she was flirting back. Just as well she was well-versed in the art of flirting with nerdy men. 'I'll come and stay with you for the weekend and we can get to know each other a little better', she said with a wink, before sending me off to my own bed. The next morning she left to deal with a family crisis after a short phone call. I made her tea and helped carry her bags, clinging to what I thought were to be the last moments I could spend with her, under the guise of help, wishing I could say something to soothe her anguish. I thought I'd never see her again.

However, in the following weeks there were e-mails, IMs and phone calls, slotted in around our lives like packing materials (if packing materials were ever more interesting than the objects they protect), and finally a 'date' was set for the visit.

In all the heady rush and excitement I realised I hadn't given a great deal of thought to what would happen if I actually got to be with this woman. What would her life-style mean for me? I had kinda thought I could flirt with impunity, that this vivacious, sexy woman, with wit, brains and a wealth of common sense was *so* far 'out of my league' that it was 'never going to happen'.

Lesson 1 – In poly, the pressure to be everything to someone is lifted. A single facet of a person can be enough.

I devoted a great deal of time trying to focus on whether I was being honest, right down to the personal

3

level, about my feelings about poly. Intellectually, I was more than fine with it. I am an anarchist at heart, and this new way of dealing with relationships seemed eminently logical. I internally role-played how it would feel for her to leave me to spend time with another lover, the worries that, compared to other partners, I wouldn't measure up (she did seem to move in a fairly intellectual crowd of very urbane, witty folk), and whether it would feel awkward to hang around with my friend after this date.

I spent a long time trying to be 'sure' before the fateful day. To be honest, in the end, and for this woman, I was sure I was going to do my damnedest not to hurt her, but still didn't know if it was going to hurt me or not.

When the long-awaited day came, it was wonderful. We talked, we loved, we dined in bed and locked the world outside to deal with its own problems. Over that weekend I learned about how she felt about me, how she had pursued *my* affections. And we talked about her current partners and my history. A few things crystallised in me, then.

Lesson 2 – I wasn't *sharing* her. She was making space in her busy life for *me*.

Lesson 3 – It was love rather than, as some cruel or uneducated people seem to continually try to suggest, 'friends with benefits'.

Now this might seem like the end of the story, but the following week I was 'invited' (some might say 'dragged') to a house party in another part of the country to meet part of her 'poly network': a collection of friends and lovers (initially, I didn't know which was which) who wanted to know all about this hermit of a man who had drawn M's eye (and, I later found out, been the cause of more than a little gushing). I went, very nervously, to meet her chosen family.

It was rather a baptism of fire. I saw her interact with friends and lovers, and was, in turn, interacted with and kissed and loved in front of them. During that party, I was confronted with, in the most personal way, what it means to be poly. Forced to acknowledge what being part of a loving group was like. With all the highs of acceptance and some of the little spikes of jealousy, in a packed house where I knew precisely one person (M herself). It was more than a little nerve-wracking. Dealing with all the new people *and* the new emotional input was incredibly stressful. I later found out that M wanted to know if I really was capable of accepting this facet of her life, before she got too attached to me. Her friends had suggested that the party was a great opportunity to do this. I now agree with them. I learned a lot that evening, too.

I came out at the other end, unscathed, with new questions and some of the answers I was looking for, and on the journey home, I fixed these nagging doubts:

Lesson 4 – Most of my remaining self-doubt was based on what other people might think. I realised I didn't much care, given that people rarely care about what I think. Once I realised I didn't care, I was fine.

Lesson 5 – I am loved by M, and am accepted by M's other partners as a part of her life.

All these 'lessons' came to me with long walks and much thinking, and were hard to come by. None of the easily available material seemed to cover my precise situation. All the books seemed to cover what happens when the reader decides *they* are poly, rather than what to do if poly comes and finds *you* out of the blue. **Hint: Don't, if you are new to poly, watch any of the sensationalised polyamory documentaries on YouTube ... If you have a specific, intelligent question, ask a poly person.**

It took real work to figure it out. I was too embarrassed at my naïveté to want to ask stupid questions, rather working it out for myself until I got stuck. I am here today to tell you it certainly was worth it. M also deserves a lot of credit for answering questions and gently shooting down some of my erroneous preconceptions.

I have since talked to my parents and close friends about polyamory, and let other acquaintances know, whenever they have enquired. It is not a secret. I explain carefully and completely whenever it is required. Many have stated, and still do, that they are 'worried' about me, and I can only hope this fades with time. I am certainly not ashamed. Instead, I am fiercely proud that a rather marvellous woman chose, and continues to choose, to spend some of her time with me.

I have also tried to comfort her through a couple of breakups between her and two other partners, including, sadly, with my friend. I was rather surprised at myself, that my concern with her pain really was more important than any 'extra' time I might get with her (I am rather cynical, sometimes, about my own motivations). I, in addition, seem to enjoy her being happy with other partners (and that one was, if possible, even more of a surprise). I guess I am lucky that all her partners are people I can honestly like.

I could go on about dealing with jealousy or the feeling that you're cheating with someone else's partner. I could happily fill pages about 'coming out' as being partners with a poly person or explaining the best way to explain polyamory to an acquaintance. Anyone that knows me would say, in their kindest hour, that I am somewhat verbose. In harsher moments, they would imply that the listener to one of my longer answers had better bring a packed lunch! But better, more qualified people would, and will, do this with much more élan and skill than I. All I can do is relay my own wonderful, and at times soul-searching, experience.

Am I now polyamorous myself? Truth be told, I don't know. If and when I find someone that I can love at the same time as M, I'm sure she'd be happy for me. I don't know if it's possible for me, but I no longer rule it out (there is very little I do rule out, these days), or worry about it. I am a stronger, more capable, broader-horizoned and, arguably, better person for the whole experience. I get the feeling that my adventures with M have only just begun, and all I need to do to continue being a part of her life is to keep being me.

The love is the most important, shiniest bit, after all.

Newish to poly
Melody

When I was barely eighteen, I met the man who would become my husband. We met at college and were friends who, nearing the end of our freshman year, fell in love. After a year of dating at school, we moved a thousand miles away, back to my hometown, to finish school. After another year, we eloped, and after another year, found ourselves unexpectedly pregnant. That pregnancy ended in a physically disabled child with autism, and my life became about parenting my child. During college, I had lived with him and three other men. One of the roommates, Chris, was my best friend, and drove across two states to witness the marriage on my behalf. I spent most of my time with Chris, and slept with Tim. Later, when it became tough for us to manage the demands of parenting a child with special needs along with another baby and things grew financially tight, I suggested our old roommate move in with us. My husband was appalled and didn't want a roommate living with us. I tried to explain the benefits of communal living from my point of view. Chris was a good cook, which would relieve the every-meal burden placed on me. Chris wanted children, but hadn't found a mate. Our children would have a live-in uncle. There would be another set of hands, another income. I brought it up to Chris and he said, "But you're married." This confused me. In college, we had been a couple, why did the marriage make all of us living together no longer an option? I was unable to convince them.

Sometime later that year, my close friend and on-again, off-again boyfriend through high school and early college, Peter, came back to our hometown during the summer. He and I met for ice cream at the local ice-cream shop and he asked me if I had ever heard of polyamory. I said I hadn't, but I could break down the word and guess that it meant "many loves" and was probably like a permutation of polygamy. He explained that was "pretty close" and said that it meant I could have more than one husband, if I wanted, and was I interested? We talked about how my current husband would never go for it. He was uptight, sexually reserved, and had always felt threatened by my relationship with Peter. Peter and I shared remorse that it was an unlikely possibility, but wished it could be so. I came home from coffee and asked my husband if he had ever heard of polyamory. He went off on a judgmental rant and I didn't continue the conversation.

Fast-forward about five years, eight and a half years years into the marriage, and my husband fell in love with his coworker. I tried to talk to him about it, but he denied it vehemently. He had been raised in a world where sex and emotions were shameful. At the same time, my career was growing by leaps and bounds and I was able to lead a much more independent life. Unfortunately, my husband chose to leave the relationship full of anger, blame, resentment, shame, guilt, and secrets rather than have an open conversation about his feelings and either open our relationship or choose to end it in a responsible manner. After more than nine years of marriage, we separated and filed for divorce.

On the very day that I decided to file divorce papers, my old friend Peter, with whom I hadn't had contact in several years, sent me a text saying he was in town, and did I want to have coffee? I texted back, "How about a beer?" We talked for hours and he said to me, "Melody, you can't see how vulnerable you are right now, but you are very vulnerable. Don't date anyone exclusively right now. Feel open and free about dating. Take your time and learn what you like. There is a lot to be learned about oneself from dating. You are going to miss having a person to talk to. Let me be that person. When you need a shoulder to cry on or to yell or scream or process, call me. I will be there." It remains one of the nicest things anyone has done for me. He was there, anytime I needed him. He was a true friend and a help with processing my life. When I joined online dating, he was open with me about how casual sex was viewed in his experience and helped me feel normal about what I was doing. His assertion that I shouldn't jump into an exclusive relationship (he warned about serial monogamy) gave me the freedom to explore and to become my own person.

After being single for about eight months, I met a man, Daniel, who said he loved me on the first date. It turned out that his wife was in the process of moving out, and I saw the vulnerability that Peter must have seen in me. I told him that I didn't date anyone exclusively and didn't want to fall into a pattern of serial monogamy, but that

I would like to see him again. I later sent him an email telling him about leaving my marriage and Peter's offer to me. I extended a similar offer to him. This man was fiercely intelligent and looked up serial monogamy online and found a polyamorous community in our small mountain town. He asked me if I had ever heard about polyamory and I told him that I had, but it had been years ago, and I didn't actually know much about it. He was already halfway through *The Ethical Slut* and read it aloud to me. Having both come out of relationships involving affairs, and being of intelligent, progressive mindsets, we were both drawn to the possibilities of poly and often daydreamed of how it could work and how we could set up our own "village."

We each set up a profile in the online community of polyamorous people in our little town. When the dropdown menu asked for my sexual orientation and included "heteroflexible" I was ecstatic. I had always been attracted to women as well as men, but only dated men and was interested in exploring. I was not yet comfortable with the label of "bisexual" because I hadn't ever confirmed I enjoyed sex with women, I just knew I wanted to try.

I recognized several women I had been to high school with on the site, and one I worked with professionally. We researched the etiquette of "outing" and I sent them all messages saying hello and asking for anonymity in public and offering the same. I also suggested getting together for coffee or lunch to talk. Slowly, my poly community grew and I had people to have theoretical discussions with. At the same time, my relationship with Daniel grew and we started to feel monogamous. Neither one of us was interested in dating outside the relationship, except theoretically. I felt like I was in danger of feeling like I was "safe" in a monogamous relationship. Monogamous thinking is hard to unlearn. I went on a date with a man who had recently opened his marriage. We had been getting along really well online and then met for dinner. There was tons of chemistry and it was exciting. I decided I would enjoy going home with him. Daniel and I had talked early on about how neither of us owned the other and we were each free to do as we wished, but I wanted to make sure that it was fine if I had some wild first-date, high-chemistry sex. I sent him a text, and I didn't hear back. It put me in a position of discovering for myself whether I chose to believe he would continue to be okay with it and whether our relationship would survive if it turned out he wasn't okay. I went home with the man and had really great sex. In the morning, I called Daniel to talk about it. The interesting thing for me about the experience was it made me feel much closer to Daniel, and made me really want to see him. We talked about it and everything was not only okay, it was better than okay. A few weeks later, he finally managed to land a date with a coworker he had been crushing on for a few years. I was excited for him. We agreed he would text me after the date so I knew how things had gone. He texted me at 2 a.m. to tell me that he was headed home. I felt both relieved that he wasn't spending the night and very sad for him that he wasn't spending the night.

Together, we explored the world of poly. Because we were beginning our relationship from that perspective, it was easier to let go of the monogamous way of thinking from a platform of scarcity. We endured many adventures together. He fell hard for a girl who didn't fall back, and was actually interested in me. I reconnected with my first girl crush from high school, Amy, and had a threesome with her and one of her partners. I enjoyed the sex with Amy more than the man and it gave me a lot to think about. Her partner (though an organizer of the poly group in town) got exceedingly possessive and jealous and ended up interrupting us in the middle of a beautiful intimate, sexual moment and demanding to have sex with both of us. (I said no.) Most notably, Daniel and I were invited by Amy to a bar late at night over Christmastime and we decided to go meet her. She was there with Daniel's old on-again, off-again girlfriend from high school, Georgia. Georgia, Daniel, and I ended up talking for hours. Amy had told her that we were poly and she was excited because she and her domestic partner with whom she had children were poly, too. She came home with us from the bar and we talked. We arranged to go out together as couples and talk. She and Daniel were so excited to reconnect and I loved watching that connection happen.

A few weeks later we all went out on a date. It was confusing for me because it started to feel like they wanted to swing. Her partner, Luke, was a photographer like I am, and wouldn't leave me alone. He wanted to show me all of his cameras and talked a mile a minute. I was crushing on Georgia and barely got to talk to her. Daniel and Georgia kept disappearing into the crowd to talk and leaving me alone with Luke. He was nice, but I was afraid I was being put in a position I wasn't ready to navigate. Daniel and Georgia reappeared and dictated that we head back to Daniel's house to talk. We carpooled back to the house and chatted until 3 a.m. Eventually they headed home. I began to talk to Georgia, who was also back in school, separately. I needed emergency childcare for my two-year-old one day and asked Luke and Georgia to take her. As I got to know Luke and Georgia better, I came to enjoy both of their friendships, and the four of us got along well. They talked about how they had been poly for over five years, but had never really acted on it. They were essentially monogamous, but would tell each other when they had crushes and each of them had been on a few dates, but neither was eager to jump into bed with anyone. Meeting a functional, loving, established poly couple really helped me feel secure in slowing down and letting relationships evolve and come to me rather than feeling the need to seek multiple relationships out. Unfortunately, Daniel experienced extreme stress and ended up needing intensive psychiatric care and ultimately he decided to take a break from dating, though he continued to stay in touch with me and considered me part of his inner circle. I was sad because he was a good friend and partner and we had joined this community together. I wasn't sure how to approach the community alone without seeming like a unicorn. A few weeks later, I had been on a terrible date and come home early. I got a text from Georgia that said, "We ended up having an impromptu get-together at our house, if you want to come over." "I will be right there," I said.

It was interesting that I reacted to the text in the way I did. It was surprisingly validating to be invited as an individual. It helped me realize that I still tied some of my worth up in my relationship status, and a new type of healing began. It had always appeared to me that Georgia and Daniel were interested in each other, leaving me with a little crush on Georgia and in sort of a theoretical metamour relationship with Luke. I arrived at the party happy to see my friends. They asked how Daniel was and I told them about my terrible date. It was a small gathering and I was enjoying a bottle of wine. It got late quickly and people started to leave. Georgia encouraged me to stay so we could talk about Daniel. Luke went up to bed and Georgia and I talked. It was late and we were tired and she invited me to crash there for the night. I went upstairs with her and crawled into their bed in my shirt and panties. I was half asleep when she rolled over and was right in front of me. We smiled and kissed each other. It was one of those kisses that can't be left at a kiss, and we began making out and exploring each other. Luke woke up and asked permission to join us. It felt right and good and turned into a lovely night. They were sweet in the morning and it was all exceptionally normal.

The next day they sent me a long note electronically apologizing for not having talked about introducing sexual intimacy to our mutual relationship before it happened. They like to be intentional about their choices and make sure that everyone is consenting. I reassured them that they hadn't taken advantage of me and that even though it came as a surprise, I was very happy.

Our relationship evolved over the next six months as all relationships do. We were friends and helped each other out. I took Luke to get his driver's license before they got their first car in years (they had been biking everywhere) and we watched each other's children. Our children became good friends naturally. I continued going on dates with men. I had one relationship with a man that started right after the first night I spent with them and he knew in the first email exchange what I had just experienced. I had two more sexual experiences with Luke and Georgia while I was dating him and eventually he decided he really wanted to partner with me and asked for some time where I was dating only him. He wanted a closed relationship and I explained to him that for me, once I had thought about poly intellectually, and experienced how healthy it was, I would never be monogamous again. I might choose to act monogamously, but I felt I identified as poly. I explained I would see our relationship as open, but with no one walking through the door. He understood this and was happy with that arrangement.

He came to Luke's birthday party and they came over for dinner. I talked to them about it and they were the most accepting, loving partners anyone could ask for. They were sad, but they understood. I felt like I was breaking up with someone because of another person's insecurities, and it didn't sit well. Eventually that relationship didn't work out and while I had stayed good friends with Luke and Georgia, it took a little while to re-establish a sexual connection. They moved to a cabin outside of town and me and my children started having a good excuse to spend the night and we found an opportunity to sleep together more frequently and we managed to go on a date and hold hands in a movie theater. We all talked about how things were moving from a fun addition to a friendship into something "more." We decided intentionally to enter a triad of sorts. Georgia had dated a couple earlier in her life and had always been made to feel secondary, and as such, they didn't want primary/secondary labels. Their goal was that we move forward in a way that would eventually allow a balanced triad. We talked about how unsure we all were about knowing how to move forward, but how it felt right and how our feelings for each other were growing. The woman and I had long known we were attracted to other women, but neither of us had ever fallen for someone same-gendered before, and how lucky we are to have an emotionally mature person to explore that with. At this point, I don't know where things will go. I enjoy my time with them out on their homestead, and when I am there, we feel like a big, happy family. I got to cut their daughter's hair for them, and our families blend nicely. I cannot move out of town at this point, so that barrier prevents us from moving too quickly. We spend two to three nights a week together and it just works.

I recently attended a comedy show where threesomes were the butt of every other joke, a fantasy to be attained and something that never really happens. I realized I have had only threesomes for months now. It is my new normal.

We are not publicly open about it, but I did start to disclose to a friend last week. The experience showed me how far from monogamous thinking I am. My friend asked if my boyfriend made it to my party. I said that I wasn't dating that guy anymore, but that my girlfriend had made it. She asked, "Girlfriend? Like a girl you are dating?" and I said, "Yes. We've been dating for about six months." She asked who and I told her and she said, "But she's married! Does he know!?!?" Technically, Luke and Georgia aren't married, but they pass. Laughing in my head at how intimately Luke was aware of the situation I simply said yes. She asked, "Why don't they just get divorced?" and suddenly I realized how unprepared I was for this conversation and how far from that type of thinking I was. I was shocked. Why would they divorce?! I simply answered back, "Why would they?" and she said that if I was dating Georgia, then obviously their relationship was over. I explained that just as she could love both of her children, Georgia could love both of us. She seemed skeptical and asked, "But what about the kids?!" and I explained that it was like any other playdate. They had lots of adults around who loved them and as far as the children knew, we were all just friends.

Ultimately, for me, that will always be true. We are really close friends and I think we always will be. I love them, as a couple, and as individuals. We talk about building me a house on the homestead in the future. We talk about communal living. We wash dishes, fold laundry, and sit around the fire and drink beer. In most ways, the time we have together is the most "normal" that my children experience. It is healthy and loving and open and accepting and evolving however we want it to or need it to.

How I arrived at being poly

Anonymous

The relationship I remember most really didn't last very long, and I don't even remember her name, but it was the first to come to my mind in response to the question someone asked about my most memorable relationship.

I was in the navy in Norfolk, Virginia, and my first wife was bedding every sailor she came across. Before I found out the extent of the problem, there was a scene and the shore patrol got involved.

I became friends with one of the members of the shore patrol, and he is the one who told me the full extent of my first wife's sleeping around. I started going to his place in navy housing to play Yahtzee. His upstairs neighbor was a nurse whose husband was out to sea, and she also played Yahtzee with us.

There was very good chemistry between us, though at that time I don't think I knew about the concept of chemistry. It was a course I took in high school, and had nothing to do with relationships. We treated each other like kids. She acted mad at me when I won a close game, and reached over and marked on my hand with her pen. Of course that set the tone and we were both marking on each other.

The next time we got together to play Yahtzee, she and I left at the same time, and spent a while talking in the parking lot. It was cold, so we went upstairs to her place to finish talking. We continued to act like kids with our fighting behavior. At one point I grabbed her wrist when she tried to hit me. At that point we sort of melted together.

She felt very guilty about cheating on her husband, but we continued to see each other anyway. That is such a euphemism, we kept having sex together. LOL. The family who we played Yahtzee with realized what was going on between us, and told me I was being no different from the sailors having sex with my wife. I felt bad, but we were in love (I didn't put that label on it at the time, but it was indeed love), and continued to see each other and to have sex. We just got more sneaky about it. We had to end the affair when her husband returned, but I think it hurt us both to do so.

I think those two events, my first wife sleeping around and my affair with the nurse, were the start of my poly mindset. I got out of the navy, went through my drug phase, and moved to California because of Scientology. I met my current wife, who was here for the same reason, and we married on our anniversary of getting together the next year.

My current wife and I both had read George and Nena O'Neill's *Open Marriage* and Robert Rimmer's *The Harrad Experiment*, which along with our previous experiences settled me firmly into the poly mindset. Although, we didn't call it poly until many years later: we just had, and still have, an open marriage. The result of this mindset was that as part of our wedding ceremony we specifically had the vows allow us to be with others.

When I proposed to her I started by asking what she needed and wanted in a second dynamic (Scientology terminology) partner. We didn't exactly match each other's ideal partner, but we were pretty close, and decided that we should marry until better partners come along. That never happened, and we are still together forty years later.

We raised our kids with full knowledge of both our polyamorous and nudist lifestyles. They even participated in my "marriage" ceremony to another woman. One of them is fully polyamorous themselves, one is grudgingly accepting of our lifestyles, and the others are fully accepting.

Diversity of love relationship concepts

Kirstin Rohwer

My two families

Viny

On the morning of October 3, 2014, I woke up to the sound of little feet padding down the hallway, and the first thought that swam to the surface of my consciousness was "I didn't lose my family over this." And I lay there in the dark, in the guest room of my sister's San Francisco apartment, listening to my three-year-old niece's cheerful chatter, feeling so overwhelmed by my good fortune that I didn't know what to do. Cry? Jump up and down on the bed, hollering "Woohoo!" in my most rambunctious voice? Light a candle and send out some love-vibes to those less fortunate than myself?

But let's back up a minute, because early-morning realizations generally don't make sense to anyone but the realizer. "I didn't lose my family over this." What does that even mean? I could change it to "I didn't lose my family over my polyamorous lifestyle," which would be accurate enough, but something in me rebels against putting it that way. The translation that feels most true to me is "I didn't lose my family over my family."

For most of my adult life, I have had two families: the family I was born into, and the family I've chosen for myself. The family I was born into includes my mother, my father, my sister, my brother, and a bunch of other people related to me by blood or marriage: aunts, uncles, cousins, you get the picture. My chosen family includes my husband of twenty-one years and the two children we decided to bring into the world together, an eighteen-year-old son and a six-year-old daughter—but it doesn't stop at neatly nuclear. There's also the man I dated for seven years. There's the woman my husband dated, and her husband, whom I dated, and their two children, all of whom will be sharing Thanksgiving dinner with us this year, a tradition we started back in 2006. There's also the amazing person I'm "pinned" to, or whatever you call it when you're married to someone else, and he's married to someone else, but you've committed to each other for the rest of your lives. There are my in-laws, of course, and also my out-laws, or whatever you call it when you get pinned to someone and his mother and father and sisters and brothers and aunts and uncles all welcome you with open arms. And there are others in my chosen family, too: a shifting web of people whose lives are intertwined with mine, some temporarily, some intermittently, but all of them important, all of them loved. It's a big family, and it keeps on growing.

Throughout my twenties and into my thirties, I tried to keep my two families—the family I was born into, and my chosen family—as separate as possible. The only points of contact between these two separate groups were myself, my husband, and our son. (Our daughter wasn't born yet.) And then one day, my son said to me, "You know, I feel like I'm getting farther and farther away from Grandma and Grandpa." When I asked him why, he explained, "Because I can't really talk to them. They wouldn't approve of our lifestyle." He was only ten years old at the time—far too young to have a "lifestyle."

It was at that point that I realized I would have to come out as polyamorous to my parents and my sister. I had already told my brother I had an open marriage, years earlier, but I had made him promise to keep this titillating tidbit to himself, and he'd been true to his word. So I came out to my mother. Then I came out to my father. Then I came out to my sister. And they did not approve. Not one little bit. My mother said, "I think your lifestyle is immoral and unethical." She wanted to make sure I understood that she had no interest in meeting any of my "extraneous" people. My father said he couldn't understand why I needed to share the sordid details of what he referred to as my "private life." The letter I wrote to my sister elicited no response until several months later, when she finally broke the silence by sending me a snail-mail reply in which she expressed concern for my son, whom she saw as the innocent victim of his parents' selfishness.

I was pretty sure I was going to lose one of my families over the other one. It was an awful feeling. It reminded me of the way I had felt way back in the spring of 1999, on the evening when my husband locked me out of our bedroom because I had lingered too long over an email I was writing to my new lover. I spent a sleepless several hours balled up on the sofa, with a slightly damp bathroom towel spread over my legs as a makeshift blanket, crying into the upholstery, berating myself, thinking I'd been naïve, I'd been stupid, I'd fucked it all up, and love had failed me. Of course, love hadn't failed me. Love never fails us. That sounds schmaltzy, I know, but it's true.

Back now to the autumn of 2014, at the end of a week-long visit with my sister and her family, right after they relocated to San Francisco from the east coast. Both my sister and her husband had just started at their new jobs, but they hadn't yet figured out a workable childcare situation, which is why I had volunteered to fly out and play nanny for a little while. My sister was extremely grateful. "After five p.m., you're off the clock," she told me. "Please don't feel like you're stuck here every night. Go out and do something fun! Doesn't your friend Scott still live in the East Bay?" My friend Scott. The man who spent seven years of his life with me. "Yes," I said, surprised she'd brought him up, and quite delighted, "he does. And it would be great to see him!"

So, Scott and I went out to dinner. We had a lovely time together, as usual. He told me, over tacos in the Mission, how much he's grown to love my husband over the years: "Remember the last time you guys all came down to visit me? I realized I wasn't just happy to see you and the kids—I was also happy to see *him!* And he was happy to see *me!* How great is that?" Ironically, he said, it wasn't until after he and I split up that he began to realize how much he valued his relationship with my husband. You should have seen the thousand-watt smile on my face at that moment. For me, there is nothing quite so wonderful as knowing that someone I love is truly appreciated by someone else I love. After dinner, Scott walked me back to my sister's place. She invited him in, we chatted together convivially for fifteen minutes or so, and then he said his goodbyes and left. It wasn't a big deal. Which is *exactly* why it felt like such a big deal.

When I woke the next morning, what dawned on me was simply this: I no longer have two families. I have *one* family. Not because I was forced to choose one family over the other, but because I stopped separating them from each other, and they chose to keep choosing me.

Long distance

Sami Peterson

Even when I am
sluiced with desire
by another
I feel red blood cells
full of you
twinkling in my currents.
More precisely,
you are the sunlight
which draws the piercing white light
on the peaks of my turbulent water
able to warm me
and touch my surfaces
and soak
in
even from far away.

Author's note: After entering my first long-distance relation-ship starting last year, I was surprised to discover how taking on new partners activates my feelings and sense of desire for my long-distance partner. Polyamory keeps her closer to me, not more estranged, as one might expect. As I continue to date my other partners, it gives me energy/excitement that I some-times bring back to her.

Becoming an unlikely unicorn triad

Katerina Stratford

From the outside we might appear to be the poly unicorn triad that lots of people fetishize at first: a married, ostensibly heterosexual couple that meets an attractive woman, turns her in to a girlfriend, and adds her to their polycule as a live-in lover. Sounds like the plot for a porn movie? Turns out real life was not exactly so predictable. To understand how we became the unlikely unicorn triad we are, you have to understand how we got here.

In my head I have always been non-monogamous, and most of my relationships have been non-monogamous in some way. Usually we would talk about it and have some ground rules that structured what we did with other people, but that came later. At first it was more fumbling and trying to figure out how to share "Vera," my best-friend-with-benefits since I was fifteen, with her boyfriend-of-the-moment. We were teenagers in love, stupid as hell. Plus no one had the idea of friends with benefits yet so we were not calling it that, just making it up as we went along.

Then I had a series of "monogamous" relationships, but I cheated on every girl I dated. I was young and stupid, my heart had not been broken yet, and I did not realize the impact that could have at that time. It never occurred to me to try to negotiate non-monogamy, until I saw an MTV special on polyamory and then I brought it up with every girl I dated. They would all say that was cheating, or they would only do it if the stars aligned on every fourth Tuesday of a leap year when the moon was in Capricorn blah blah blah. So that never worked out, or it would work for a while but then drama around lying and cheating would inevitably destroy everything.

Eventually I got my heart broken by a girlfriend who had always said no to all of the other women I wanted to sleep with, only to turn around and sleep with one of those women herself. I was devastated, and it made it really hard for me to trust people after that. I thought about how I had done the same thing—not exactly the same thing, but I had lied to people and they found out about it and that was how they felt, the way I felt right then. I understood it on a different level once karma had kicked my ass, and I began to pay a lot more attention to how I affected other people. It made me realize how my cheating and forcing non-monogamy on others had felt.

After that I committed myself to monogamy because it seemed to be the only choice at the time. I had brought up non-monogamy with everyone I was dating, and they all hated the idea. Eventually I ended up falling hard for a girl who rescued me from a terrible situation. In classic Nightingale fashion, I fell for my knight in shining armor (or Nikes and basketball shorts, in this case). Turns out, once the flush of the drama wore off, we did not really complement each other well in real life. Even though we did not last long, at the time I was committed to actually being monogamous with her because I had felt that special kind of pain that comes from someone lying and cheating on you, and I was determined not to do that to anyone else ever again.

A short-lived relationship with a woman who acted non-monogamously but would not call it that, and would not discuss it openly, was weirdly like dating an earlier version of myself. It made me decide to be single because I clearly had to learn about myself and progress as a person, so I could figure out what a healthy relationship would be for me. For the next two years I had small flings with people, nothing serious, and was pretty much single. I focused on dealing with my own mental health issues, facing an addiction that had been nagging me, and growing up on the inside. Over time I realized how important trust and honesty were for me, and that they had to form the basis of any relationship if it was going to go anywhere. I also came to understand that I could not reasonably expect any single person to meet all of my needs.

In the middle of all of this, I was traveling with my job and met "David," who was a pleasant coworker and all-around nice guy. Having discovered a mutual fascination with *Doctor Who*, David invited me over to his place to watch TV. While I was over there hanging out in the Whoverse, David's wife, "Anne," breezed through the room on her way in from work, barely even registering my presence. I, on the other hand, noticed her. A lot. Very a lot. It's a thing! Anyway, I was smitten.

A couple of days later David texted me something vaguely flirty, to which I saucily responded, "Your wife has a better chance." David responded, equally saucy, "Good luck with that." Later that day I wrote Anne to tell her I had a crush on her, and she was charmed by my awkward straightforwardness. We started hanging out, making out, and fell for each other quickly.

In what felt like months but was actually only about three weeks, Anne and I bonded with devotion, having fun and snogging constantly. Things were going pretty well in honeymoonville, with none of the challenges that real life brings at the surface just yet, when circumstances drew me away and I had to leave Anne and David's house to return to work. Reluctantly finding myself in a long-distance relationship, I missed Anne terribly. We talked every day and Anne came to visit me a couple of times, which helped a lot. I also had several flings during this time with other people who all knew about each other. It was awesome! For the first time I had a functioning primary relationship, work was good, and while I missed Anne a lot, I could talk to her and we could work things out by communicating with each other more smoothly over time. Everything was looking up for me.

Then, out of the blue, my beloved grandmother's death threw me for serious a loop. My grandmother was the woman who raised me and loved me like a mother when her daughter (my mom) turned out to be a bit wacky. OK, pretty much batshit crazy, but I digress. What you need to know is that this woman was the bedrock of family love for me, the safe haven when my mom was off on another tangent or whatever. Out of my entire messed-up family, my grandmother was the one person I could trust, the only person who ever really had my back. My grandmother meant the world to me and, when she died, Anne was there to catch me. And I fell apart. I mean *completely* fell apart. Anne rode the waves and gave me tissue, fed me ... and became my family.

So now we come full circle to where we began. I am back at Anne and David's place, and we are trying to figure out how to live as a family. They have space upstairs, and I have my own private space downstairs. Anne is a bi-level traveler, spending some nights in one bedroom and other nights in the other.

We are still figuring out how to share space, have boundaries, and meet everyone's needs. Sometimes it is complicated and uncomfortable, and sometimes it is a ton of fun with love for everyone. Kind of like many other families, or at least like the lucky ones who really love each other.

Part II: This is what a poly family looks like

On letting our poly family take shape

Juliette Siegfried

When Roland and I first opened up to polyamory, it was my big idea. After all, I was the one with a penchant for falling in love with multiple people and thus cheating on the men in my life at the time. Roland believed in my (and everyone's) ability to love more than one person at a time, and he supported me being authentic with both him and with other men in my life. But at the time, he himself didn't see the need to have any additional relationships beyond me. So, for the first seven or eight years of our open marriage, we always expected to find another man to be with, preferably as another primary for me, and as a friend for him.

In fact, I dated many men over those years, but none of them seemed interested in joining us as part of a family, and frankly now that I look back, none of them would have been suitable. In 2005 we had a big surprise, as Roland found a poly girlfriend. We had started a Yahoo group on polyamory with the intention of meeting other likeminded people, and she was the very first to sign up. Her name was Nina, and she had an eight-year open relationship of her own. We were delighted to meet another couple that shared our odd views on love and relationships, and soon Roland and Nina clicked.

It was an educational and intense experience for all of us. Until then, it was just me dating, and wishing he had someone so he'd understand what it was like for me. At the same time, I didn't want to pressure him into something he didn't want. This relationship evolved naturally, and was brief—but intense. It was a wonderful way for him to understand my perspectives better, such as how it was for me having a boyfriend. In particular, it was a great way for him to understand the pressure of New Relationship Energy, and the challenges of always meeting our agreements in terms of safe sex. One night in particular, I remember him stumbling back to our apartment, hair all askew, a bit shell-shocked, but very, very happy. He hadn't had any intoxicants other than a passionate night with Nina. He struggled greatly to tell me that they had not been careful with condoms that night, and from then on he was a bit softer with me on such important topics.

The relationship only lasted a few months, and he still didn't see himself as needing more relationships, so I continued my search for my "second husband."

We met Laurel in 2007 in Spain. She was in a poly relationship with a friend of ours, but that relationship was waning. She and Roland (and I) hit it off brilliantly, and soon Roland was involved in his second poly relationship, and I had a wonderful new friend. Neither Laurel nor I is bisexual, so our relationship is platonic. I was jealous of her for a couple of weeks, but as I got to know her it became clear that she shared our fundamental values of an open family, committed but never closed to the possibility of new love. She didn't want to take Roland from me; in fact I sensed she would feel as stifled as I would in a closed monogamous relationship with anyone. I also quickly got over my fears that she was "perfect" in every way. She was human, just like me, and my jealousy soon evaporated.

Before long, it became clear that the three of us hoped for the same kind of life, living together yet being open to love when it came along. So much for me finding a second husband! We were now a MFF, V-style triad. Seven years later, we still laugh about the fact that Roland and I were looking so hard for "the right guy," and the configuration we never even seriously considered is the one that worked out so well for us in the end.

I see so many poly couples (and singles, in fact), searching for something specific. Usually it's a particular configuration (often a woman to complete the couple), but also other configurations, just like we were. Whenever asked, I counsel these folks to remain open to the possibilities. You just never know in the end what might really work for you. And you might miss out on something amazing if you close yourself off to certain outcomes. Obviously, if you're not gay or bi you can't pretend you are—I'm not suggesting that. Nor can you fake romantic love. But I guess what I see as most important is staying open to the possibilities that friendship offers in a poly relationship. Often, people seem to insist on romantic love between everyone involved. I suggest that friendship and intimacy can co-exist with or without romantic love, and in fact opening up to friendship might allow the blossoming of a wonderful family you never imagined.

Since joining with Laurel, we have also joined with Barry, her older friend of over twenty-five years. He is not romantically involved with any of us, but due to his extensive relationship with Laurel, and generally being an easy guy to get along with, he is now a full-fledged member of our family and a dear grandfather figure to our five-year-old daughter, Maya. This is, to me, what polyamory is really about: openness to all the facets of family and love, not just the romantic ones, and to forming committed bonds that improve life for everyone involved. We're sure happy with how things worked out!

A (not so ordinary) day in the life of a poly activist

Maxine Green

It's painfully early in the morning, and we have been up for hours already. I do not even want to think about how early it is, but as the three of us hop out of our cab at the TV studio my mind is already racing with all of the things I want to say. The points I *have* to make, and the ones I will try to slip in if I can. All three of us are well aware that the presenters of the show will have their own preconceived ideas about what polyamory is, and will try to spin some sort of 'drama' out of our real lives—after all, the line I had 'sold' the producers when negotiating to go on the show was the tabloid headline 'These Three Women Are ALL Dating The Same Man!' No matter.

Looking at the two women on either side of me, I feel pretty calm. Both of these women were personal friends even before we became metamours, before they became part of my extended poly family. Both of them are down-to-earth, good-natured and courageous people, and I can't think of many folks I would be prouder to stand beside. We have good reason to be here, too. For the last few years, with help from friends and various members of my poly family, I have been running an outreach event where poly people meet, greet and educate folks about what polyamory actually is, and the intricacies of ethically non-monogamous relationships. We have had a tough year though, financially, and the money we are being paid for this interview could be the difference between success and failure for the event. Jemima is also promoting her recently published book of interviews with other poly people across the UK, which she will also be selling at Polyday. As long as we get to mention these things, we figure no publicity is bad publicity.

Inside the TV studio, all is frantic. We are rushed into the same makeup room as a number of other people who will be appearing on the show, and the makeup artist sizes us up. I did my own makeup before leaving the house this morning, so apparently all I need is a quick dab of foundation on top of the powder I'm already wearing, and then I'm good to go. As we emerge from the cloud of brushes, sponges, paints and powders, a friendly elderly woman says hello to us in the corridor outside and introduces herself as the 'agony aunt' who will be on the show with us later. Jemima, Eunice and I share a look. This is the first curveball of the day. We had expected that it would just be the three of us talking to the presenters of the show. Nobody had mentioned an 'agony aunt'. Would that mean less time to try to get our point of view across? Still, she seemed friendly enough. As she bustles off down the hall a couple of other minor celebrities also pass by. It all seems a little surreal that we are deemed 'interesting enough' to be here, just because we have a slightly different attitude to relationships.

We don't get much time to think, though. The TV studio is a chaotic-looking but efficient machine, designed to hurry people along, out and through. Dizzying and dazzling and eating people alive. Everyone is friendly, cheerful and welcoming, presenters and staff alike. None of us, though, is naïve enough to believe that everyone here is 'on our side'. We are all three of us aware that the studio's goal is simple: they are there to entertain the viewers. Educating people, promoting our projects, presenting our own views? That part is the challenge we have to meet. Before too long, we have been 'processed' through the bowels of the TV studio, and are sitting on the couch in front of the cameras, being introduced. The presenters are kind enough to mention both Polyday and Jemima's book as a part of our introductions, so at the very least our main goal has been achieved and we have let the UK know that our event exists, but then comes the 'circus'.

It seems that the presenters, or the producers, or whoever decides the way the show is supposed to go, have decided that the three of us are 'victims', being taken advantage of by this mysterious man we are all seeing. The middle-aged male presenter asks this of us with an expression of fatherly concern, and it is all the three of us can do not to fall about laughing, picturing our mutual sweetheart—a sweet-faced and adorably nerdy boy of twenty-something (younger than both Eunice and myself) who is so utterly guileless he can't even manage to tell a white lie—as a manipulative harem builder. The presenters are clearly experienced at keeping the conversation flowing to the point where it is really rather tricky to actually find a space in which to speak, but when we can sneak a word in edgeways, we try to explain that we all three have secure relationships with other partners, and are still open to the possibilities of dating other people as well. The presenters are on a roll already though, and have

clearly decided that our relationships are all 'doomed'—
and bring in the agony aunt to 'prove' it.

Well into her seventies, the agony aunt is a painted
dragon of a woman who has outlived at least two husbands,
and despite her friendliness in the corridor, seems to have
been especially asked to give us a hard time. She proclaims
that our adventures in multiple romantic attachments
will 'all end in tears' . . . as though monogamous relationships somehow end any other way? She tuts, she rolls her
eyes, she practically wrings her hands in the manner of
a Shakespearian tragedy, and declares that every single
person who ever wrote to her in a polyamorous relationship was already on the road to ending badly. Eunice very
reasonably attempts to point out that 'You are an agony
aunt. People who are in *happy* polyamorous relationships
aren't going to be writing to you, by definition', but this
fails to cut off the flow of judgement. (*Had I been a little
bitchier, I might perhaps have pointed out that the failure of
their relationships indicated that she had also failed in her job
as a 'relationship adviser', no?*) Polyamory, you see, at least
according to the presenters of this show, is something
attempted by foolish young people with no serious job or
life commitments, before they learn to settle down and
become 'proper' monogamous grown-ups . . . or is it? The
female presenter of the show makes a comment about how
you don't see older people with 'proper' jobs or children on
these shows talking about polyamory, and I finally snap. I
will not be talked over any further, so I verbally elbow my
way back into the conversation and demand to be heard.

You see, in the UK, as in many other parts of the world,
there is no formal legal protection for polyamorous
people. Being 'out' is not so easy if you are concerned

about losing your job, your home, or even your children, or having to fight to protect them in court, simply because you have more people in your family than our cultural norm. Do poly families with permanent homes, jobs and children exist? Of course they do (and I am sure you'll be reading plenty more about them in the rest of this book). Some of our own partners come into exactly this category. Eunice and I both have loved ones in our lives who have children, even though we each have none of our own. We each have partners in their forties and more. We are close friends with people who are older and more settled even than we are. And many of us are 'out' to friends, family, even employers. They just can't necessarily afford to be here shouting about their relationship statuses on TV. It isn't polyamory that is only for the young and carefree, I explain, but *activism*.

I talk fast and loud, trying to cram as much information as I can into a short, precise burst, knowing that I might not get another chance. All the while knowing that this is a LIVE show. This is my opportunity to have my say properly, without fear of being edited (all three of us have experienced having our words twisted and edited in journalistic interviews and 'documentaries' and had come here hoping we could present a different view—even in a live show, it turns out, this is difficult. The producers, the presenters, the other 'guests' they bring on, each still have their own preconceived ideas of what polyamory means, and it is difficult getting through that obstacle course of errors to actually convey how things really are.

The rest of the interview passes in something of a blur. We are shuffled back into the studio after a break to hear some judgemental letters from the audience, and the presenters are more careful this time not to give us even the slightest opportunity to respond as we would have liked to. We are talked over even harder this time, but essentially we have already done what we set out to do. We have made a few more people in the world aware of the existence of polyamory. We have told people where they can go to find more information—if you are in the UK, come to Polyday!—and I have managed to squeeze in a rant that I remain proud of to this day. We are all feeling pretty pleased with our 'girls' day out'. Winding down in the green room, Eunice discovers a dozen or so messages from random guys hitting on her over the Internet (because poly girls are easy, right?), and we all have a wry chuckle at it before heading home for a nice cup of tea. My inbox, on the other hand, is full of emails from partners, friends and family, including a lovely one from my longest-standing partner's grandmother, an awesome woman in her nineties and thus older and wiser than the 'agony aunt' who so rolled her eyes at the three of us. All of these emails say effectively the same thing: 'Congratulations on not punching that horrible judgemental old woman!' One of them even calls me 'dignified' (for anyone who has never read my webcomic, I can assure you this is not usually the case).

Getting home, I catch up on my American Boy's blog, read up on what's going on around the world in terms of polyamory activism, and begin writing up my experiences for *Polytical*, the UK's poly activist online magazine. On second thought, perhaps this is a relatively normal day after all. For some families, a normal day is sitting at home watching TV and talking about what they did at school, or work, or at the shops. For my family, a normal day is talking about how we can make the world better for folks like us, and then acting on it. Some days it feels more like being a part of a league of superheroes.

Right now, though, it feels like going home to a cuddle and a cup of tea. And who doesn't want that?

Honesty helps to ride the emotional rapids

Ryan

I've only been active for about two years, so take what I share with a grain of salt. When I started being involved in the poly community, I wanted to make sure I came out to my immediate family and close friends. Thankfully, they were all very welcoming of it, and in fact, the din of hecklers in my head was ten thousand times worse than their actual reaction. I'm very much a weirdo in other aspects of my behavior and lifestyle, so I guess it didn't seem really odd to them that I would be polyamorous.

Anyway, I'm currently in a quad, with Peter, Barbie and Scarlet (names changed to protect the twisted), and there are no children in the mix, so I can't speak on that particular subject. I will say, however, that in my opinion, people that say polyamory is "bad for children" are looking at the wrong part of the map. I don't think that how the parents choose to structure their romantic relationships alone determines what is "bad for children." To me, it seems that in the "bad for children" category, "polyamorous parents" would be superseded by "malnutrition," "neglect," "abuse," etc. So long as the relationship(s) is (are) relatively harmonious and ethical to provide a healthy model for the kid(s), whether it's polyamorous or not is immaterial.

Going back to my poly family, we met at a cuddle party, and we just connected. We all agreed there was something substantial to this and wanted to explore it further. After a few more social events, I started going to their house for dinner on Sundays. Peter and Scarlet had been together for seven years at that point, and Barbie entered the picture maybe two weeks before I did. So our start was a bit wibbly-wobbly timey-wimey (putting it mildly). Peter was also struggling with an alcohol addiction at the time, and some of his behavior tripped some of Barbie's and Scarlet's triggers, so it was tough to get any solid footing. The timing of how Barbie and I entered the relationship provided an interesting jealousy dynamic in a "from all sides" kind of way. I'm only romantically involved with Scarlet; although Barbie and I explored that for a few weeks, we both decided that we're not a good match.

The drama really settled once Peter got sober and Scarlet got settled with her bipolar medication. Even then, it took me a while to really settle into the four of us being a family. Even with the rough start, I knew without a doubt that I wanted to be involved, but being a family is something else. I really dig that we're getting to that stage where we have a cauldron of inside jokes and I love that I get to see the silly things they only do in the privacy of their own home. I'm pretty sure we're about two steps away from creating our own gibberish, too.

I always cringe when I see the phrase "doing poly right/wrong," because I inevitably get on a soapbox about self-determinism and self-identity, so I'm going to segue awkwardly into pitfalls to avoid. One that I have—and I realize other people may not have this issue—is passively closing myself off when I get comfortable in a situation. So I found a way to continue being actively vulnerable by starting a podcast with Scarlet called *Honest, Open and Vulnerable*; we use topics we're interested in to tangentially talk about mental health issues we deal with. It's been therapeutic for both of us in a way that traditional therapy couldn't; we also talk about wrongfully stigmatized topics (mental health, addiction, polyamory, LGBTQ) to help stimulate a more open and compassionate conversation (at least in our little corner of the interwebs).

That was more a life-in-general pitfall, but it does tie in with polyamorous relationships in that it's more difficult if you're not being honest with what you're feeling and the headspace you're in. Granted, being honest and vulnerable doesn't automatically make poly easy, but it sure helps smooth the road a bit. I know that the process of self-investigation isn't easy or fun (well, sometimes it is), but that's the best nugget of advice I have based on my experience.

Life in the middle

Aoife Lee

I live in the middle. In reflecting on this, I realize I always have. I love everyone, and I want everyone to love me. It is my great strength ... and my downfall. I want to make everyone that I love happy all the time. It has taken me years to learn to include myself in that list ... and even more years to move myself up that list to the point that I might come first (or even close to first). I am still working on it, thankfully with the help of my family.

I am in the middle in my family. There are three of us. I have been married for five years, to the person who is my best friend, my confidant, my safe space, my refuge. Don't get me wrong—he can drive me crazier than most people on earth, but we have learned to talk (and laugh) through those moments. We have learned to talk sooner rather than later—it helps. We have been together through first experiences of non-monogamy, dating other people, and concurrent serious relationships. He has held me up during difficulties in other relationships, and I have worked to understand his envy when I had the kind of relationship he wanted to have with another. He held my hand (literally and figuratively) through the decision to sever ties with a former partner, a process that was in the interest of my own health, but broke my heart. He can make me laugh like a loon. He can sit beside me in silence with a book all afternoon. He introduced me (directly and by extension) to all the people who make up the intentional family and community that also hold me up. My life is shinier because of the day we first locked eyes.

I am in the middle in my family. There are three of us. I have been dating my sweetheart for six months. I fell hard. Surprised the crap out of me. I should know by now that this is my pattern. Like the day I met my husband, my brain could not have been further from thinking about romance the day I met her. Walking in the door after a very long workday, all I wanted was a shower and some time in silent solitude. But there was someone sitting in the kitchen with B. Poor girl, I barely said hello, I was in such a rush to get to the shower. It was only after several more evenings of hanging out at the house that I noticed her, and only when she admitted that she had a crush on me that I really considered it. Brave girl. How could I resist someone who was willing to be so authentic with me, to tell me what she was thinking and ask for what she wanted (I'm a therapist, it's our kryptonite!).

At first, we were dating long distance. I hate it, but it has its advantages when you are trying to manage multiple relationships. Being apart was horrible—I wanted to put my arms around her daily, more so on days that either of us was feeling stressed. But we were both living our independent lives, though in constant contact (thank you, twenty-first century telecommunications). If I am completely honest, I am potentially easier to be in a relationship with long distance. As a professional who tends to work more hours than most sane others (fortunately I love my job), I have little free time. Long distance allows for bursts of communication in moments between work commitments, but may disguise the fact that I work a twelve-hour day and then am exhausted.

Things happened—life always surprises us. Living together, meaning J moving into the home I have shared with B for over five years, had been put on the table as an option early on, but as a long-term plan. B and I had talked about this, and he expressed that he was content with that, and willing to express any hesitations should they occur. When difficulties in J's life arose, coming to our home in the short term was something B and I were happy to offer. As life began to calm, we realized that at least for the foreseeable future, this was/is going to be our living situation. So we have to learn to live together, to share a home, a living space, time, meals…all those difficult little things.

I am in the middle in my family. There are three of us, and I am the only one with a romantic relationship with both others. I am deeply in love with both of my partners. In some ways, they have much in common. In others, they could not be more different. In some ways, I want to make sure that I treat them each exactly the same, in the interest of fairness. However, this generally will not meet their differing needs, nor will it meet my needs. So for example, sleeping arrangements. We don't all sleep together. While I would be quite happy in the middle of that sandwich (though it would be super WARM—they are both little space heaters!), that is not comfortable and safe for each of my partners. So we alternate nights—one night I sleep in our room upstairs with B, the next night I sleep in our room downstairs with J. So what do I do on a night when I really want to sleep in a particular location? How do I say "You know, I really want to sleep upstairs on the memory foam and in the cooler room tonight..." and still try to make sure that everyone is completely happy? How do I deal with a specific request from one of them, which I am happy to make a change around, but might hurt the other? You see, I am in the middle...

Sometimes being in the middle is a great thing. Coming home from a long day at work and walking into the middle of one partner making dinner and another handing me a cup of tea and telling me to go get out of my work clothes. That's a great middle. Hosting a party for all of our friends, kissing each of my loves at midnight on New Year's, and then watching them hug and smile at one another, not lovers but great friends. That's a great middle. Even on the occasions that there is an argument—of late, being in the middle of the three of us each trying to help the other dyad hear one another has been a helpful, though difficult, experience.

Sometimes being in the middle feels like being torn in two. Knowing that both of my partners are in pain, that they each need to process that pain away from one another, and trying to prioritize who to go to first. That middle is excruciating. Learning that something that I love in one partner is irritating to the other is always difficult. Even little things contribute to this—who wants what for dinner is harder with three than with two... and it wasn't easy with just two.

Being in the middle means being caught between their needs, but also between their needs and my own. How do

I remember to ask myself what I want when I am already trying to identify and juggle their competing needs? I know that I tend to forget. Unfortunately for my poor partners, I tend to ignore my personal needs in favor of the needs of work, others, partners, etc. until I reach the point of desperation. And then don't react calmly to requests of even the most minor nature.

Returning home after a long workday, often the thing I want most is to not talk to anyone for at least an hour. I love the way that J greets me when I get home—"Hello, girl," in the same way that she has said it ever since we were first flirting. In a tone that conveys somehow that I have made her day simply by being there. B is more reserved. He has learned that perhaps my spirit animal is the hermit crab. That to really get me to come out of my shell, I am best ignored. Well, not ignored, but left to myself until all vestiges of social exhaustion and over-thinking have passed, and I am finally tired of the solitude. And he is good at keeping himself entertained while I recuperate. He has learned patience over the course of our years together. I realize it now only in the reflection from my new relationship, but this cannot have been easy for him. As J's need for reassurance and company at the end of the day battles with my need for solitude, his patient silence often gets lost in the mix. And then I worry that I have missed a need he might have.

Of course poly means being in the middle of communication a lot. Reflecting on how often I have offered this advice to others, I am sometimes embarrassed by the ways in which we continue to struggle. We are all learning to speak each other's languages, and realizing that these all differ immensely. Conversations between my very contextual self and my very concrete partner are often as clear as a bell to each of us...and as clear as MUD to the other. Because we genuinely associate different concepts with words, there can be complete agreement over what was *said*, but hours of fighting over what was *meant*. We have the willingness to communicate; we are just struggling to work out the means. And while my other partner is often a good middle ground in understanding us both, because we are not all in a romantic relationship together, intervention at that moment risks being rejected because the other is "getting into something that doesn't concern their relationship."

I am in the middle in my family. There are really six of us—three adult humans, and now three dogs too. Even that is not easy. Each of us has the dog that is more "their" familiar, and as a result the dog for whom we worry and advocate most. I'm sure that having children is more difficult, but sometimes it feels like blending families in that way!

So I am in the middle in my family. I cannot tell you how much joy I take in this. I feel so fortunate to experience so much love on a daily basis. To sit between them on the couch, leaning on one and holding the other's hand. To plan journeys together, date nights apart, family nights together. There is little that I would not do to keep that. I know that it is difficult. I know that I am not always good at it. I get tired. I get rigid. I get preoccupied. But I continue to work on it. I pressure myself to listen, to restrain my defensiveness so that I can hear what they need me to hear. It is work. It is worth it. It will always be worth it.

I hope that they both feel that way. I fear that they may not. As the connecting point and the only one who has a romantic relationship with each, I live in terror that what we all have together will somehow stop meeting their individual needs. I understand that needs change—that there might come a day when one of them needs more from me than they are getting now. I pray that I will be able to find those resources somewhere, because I cannot bear to contemplate having to let go of any of this love.

What do polyamory, infertility, healing and pole dancing have in common? Answer: Me!

Kitty Chambliss

Please allow me to introduce myself. My name is Kitty Chambliss. I am a polyamorous, married woman who happens to be an infertility survivor, as well as a pole fitness dancer who is incredibly joyous, inspired and happy with my life and where I am at, now that I find myself in my mid-forties. I am an advocate for the choice for all human beings to have the option to live traditional or alternative lifestyles if they so choose, without discrimination. I myself live an alternative lifestyle in that I live an ethically non-monogamous life. I live with both my husband of eight years and my boyfriend of four years, and our two cats. It is an unusual, charming and often-times challenging choice. But for me, it has been less of a choice, and more a statement about who I am inside.

I came to the polyamorous lifestyle somewhat by accident, but looking back, I was always polyamorous but did not know this lifestyle was available to me. I grew up in a Catholic school setting, being taught that sex was dirty and only for procreation, that masturbation was strictly forbidden, and that homosexuals were sexual deviants and therefore "going to hell." I have spent much of my adult life undoing the damage that was done by this teaching in my formative years. It wasn't until high school and college that I really started to question these teachings as not fitting my belief system and who I was becoming.

I considered myself a "cheating serial monogamist" for much of my dating life in my twenties and beyond, and eventually developed a distaste for the lies, secrecy and feeling of not being authentic that went along with it. When I met my husband-to-be, we both agreed that our previous NON-ethical non-monogamy (aka "cheating") was a behavior that we no longer wanted to engage in. We decided to manage our relationship and later our marriage how we saw fit, and not necessarily along the lines of what we felt society dictated that we do. If it felt good and healthy to us, we were going to write our own rules.

Eventually, a good friend introduced me to a book called *The Ethical Slut*, which is regarded by some as the "Bible" of polyamory. I was deeply moved by the writings in this book, and shared it with my husband. It was quite exhilarating! We felt that we had finally found a text that described who we were, who we wanted to be and how we saw our lives possibly unfolding.

And unfolded they have, and in a very non-traditional way. We tried to lead the traditional life, at least somewhat. Shortly after we were married, my father fell ill to cancer. He passed away months later after many failed surgeries, much heartache, and many, many tears. I was completely devastated. I felt ill-prepared to deal with the grief of losing a cherished family member. I found I had a hole in my heart that has never fully healed.

Several years later, we decided to start making a family, to carry on our collective family line. At that point in my life, almost all of my close friends had been married and had young children. We decided maybe it was time to follow the herd. And the thought of seeing my father in our offspring filled me with renewed hope and joy. Sadly and rather tragically for us, we found out that we were infertile. Even a team of doctors and an entire clinic could not figure out how to make me pregnant with our genetic material. And it cost a small fortune just to even get to the point of absolute failure to find all of that out. Again, I was devastated.

Then my mother started to deteriorate from dementia, diabetes and cancer as well. We spent many months helping care for her, finding her a place to live, selling my childhood home to fund it, all while watching my mother deteriorate until finally, she passed away as well. I had no family above me or below me. No parents. No children.

I needed to heal. Big time. Around this time, I started going to therapy. Also around this time, I met my boyfriend. And my healing began. It was a long, slow process ... of self-discovery, introspection, confusion, pain, revelation, elation, joy and jealousy, an entire multitude of both emotions and personal growth. I found that by creating my own unusual family, finding love in untraditional places, I was slowly healing myself. I also realized that being infertile can have its advantages: great spontaneous sex! Between talking to my therapist, and experiencing joy in multiple, loving relationships, my little world was slowly getting better. And little by little, the awful fog of depression, sorrow and anger was lifting. It did take many years though. Later I found that by writing about my experiences: the good, the bad, the ugly, of both infertility and ethical non-monogamy, not only was I helping heal myself, creating my own self-discovery awareness campaign, I was also helping heal and offer much-needed advice to others (via my blog, *Loving Without Boundaries*). It was like magic! By helping others, I helped myself, and vice versa. What a bloody miracle!

Another outlet and surprisingly healing vehicle that I discovered around this time was pole fitness dancing. My close friend—the one that had introduced me to *The Ethical Slut*, actually—thought it might be fun to take a pole dancing class. We signed up partly as a simple way for us to have a giggle, and to spend more time together. I never expected it to go anywhere beyond the silliness of taking a few classes. But once we started to learn how to do some sexy spins, impressed ourselves with our physical feats of daring, and eventually started climbing upside down on the poles, keeping up with all of the twenty-somethings in the class like a couple of crazy "cougar champs," we were hooked! I found that by overcoming my own perceived physical impossibilities (defying gravity on the pole, for example), I was able to create more confidence as well as inner and outer strength that I could then use in ALL areas of my life. My healing started to increase exponentially, and my feelings of depression and hopelessness started to lessen. And I now sing the praises of pole dancing to anyone who will listen.

Over time, as I decided to live a more authentic life, I started "coming out" to my close friends and family members one by one as a polyamorous woman who pole dances in her spare time. I hoped that they would continue to accept me and love me, even though I was following a very nontraditional path. I was leading quite an unusual life that they may not be able to fully understand, just like they could not fully understand the traumas that I had been through with all of the loss of not only my parents, but my unborn children. Overall, I found some acceptance, definitely love, but not a lot of understanding, or even the desire to understand. Most people like to change the subject away from both infertility and polyamory. It seems they want to pretend that both do not exist.

Well, I'm here to tell you that not only do they both exist, they will increase to exist. I believe both will be much more prevalent in years to come. Adults are getting married later and later in life, following career paths and starting families much later, sometimes after their best fertile years have sadly passed. And the divorce rate is still quite high, at about fifty percent of all marriages ending in failure, quite often instigated by one spouse cheating on the other, and the ensuing devastation of that. People don't understand that there is another way. I'm here to tell them there IS another way, if they decide that it may be right for them and their life.

I have also become an advocate for anti-suicide campaigns. There are droves of LGBT young people who feel they are misunderstood, ridiculed and forgotten, and they can't cope. Many sadly choose to end their life. Why is there so much intolerance in the world for those who are not like us? Those who are suffering, sometimes from mental illness or being emotionally distraught? Why can't we learn to help each other more? We NEED each other.

That is clear to me now. As my strength and confidence grew, I eventually started my own business. Helping anti-suicide campaigns is one of my greatest and most self-satisfying accomplishments to date, as well as doing creative work helping others find and do work that they love—work that inspires them and helps them come alive.

I have found my new purpose in life. It is to help my fellow person, regardless of relationship choice, age, family lifestyle, heritage, race, social status or whatever else separates us from each other. I want more joy and happiness not only in my life, but in the lives of everyone on this spinning blue rock. Earth would be such a better place every second of every day if we could all just "show up" with an attitude of generosity and gratitude, and acceptance for one another. Would you like to join me? I hope to walk beside you, and cheer you on.

Open relationships and the fear of a better match

Wilrieke Sophia

Open relationships often get the stigma that the partners involved are sexually very liberal, sharing their juices with many people. Often there is a negative energy surrounding the topic. That changes once people get to know what an open relationship really is about. Many couples I know realized that after I told them what an open relationship comes down to, they have a relationship themselves that can be labeled open is some way.

To me, an open relationship is a relationship in which you support your partner to completely and totally live the life they wish for themselves. To discover who they are, to connect with people without limitations, fears or feelings of guilt. To enjoy life to the fullest and to be the happiest person they can be.

Maybe you love dancing when your partner doesn't like it at all. You could go dancing together. Probably your partner is consciously or unconsciously sabotaging your night of fun by having negative feelings. You will notice that and not have such a great night yourself either. Maybe your partner really likes fishing. You could join him, sitting quietly at the water, staring at the float and not enjoying yourself at all.

What if you could choose to invite other people who are really compatible with the things you wish to do? It's rather impossible for one person (i.e., your partner) to match you in all your fields of interest. Why would you compromise and only do things together with your partner, when there are so many people existing who are a perfect match for the things your partner doesn't like and who would be happy to join you?

Probably you realize that you already do have matches other than your partner for certain activities. Maybe you like to go shopping with the girls, go jogging with a colleague or have a weekly chat over a cup of tea with your neighbor. And your partner is very happy for you to have these other people in your life, so s/he doesn't have to do things s/he doesn't like.

Now sit tight: I believe that is what an open relationship is all about. Find the perfect matches for you, so you can enjoy the things you want to experience in the best possible way.

Inviting new people into your life.

By saying out loud that you open up your relationship, you will find that you will open up from inside. I realized that when Sebastiaan and I decided to open up our relationship, nothing really changed within our relationship. I didn't jump the first guy I saw, he didn't jump the first cute girl he met. What I realized was that I was able to be open to new connections on a whole new level. Sebastiaan never held me back in any way, but I did hold back myself. I had many limiting thoughts making me afraid that I would do something wrong. That I would hurt somebody, especially my partner.

When we opened up, I could let go of these fears. Since there was nothing I could do accidentally wrong, there was nothing to worry about. I felt so much love flowing through me. Now I didn't have to push it away anymore, but I could share it with people. I didn't have to limit this love to my partner and kids. The funny thing about love is that the more you share of it, the more there is available.

New people started appearing in my life. Amazing people, with lots of love to share from an open heart. We could create an instant connection of love, since none of us held back. We could hug, cuddle and kiss and feel very loved. My partner could only be happy for me, since the amount of love I was feeling multiplied, and I showered him with all of that. No complaints whatsoever. ☺

What if I like a new connection better?

A question I receive often is this one: "If I have an open relationship, won't chances of me and my partner splitting up increase since I could easily meet someone I like better than my partner? Or worse, won't my partner leave me since s/he will find a better match?"

In whatever type of relationship you are, you always meet new people when you are open to it. There is always a chance you will meet someone you like very much. Especially when you are in a long-term relationship, the spark and excitement a new connection bring can be very attractive.

In a monogamous relationship you are not allowed to openly explore this exciting new connection. That leaves you with three options: ignore your feelings, secretly go after your feelings, or leave your partner and go for this new connection.

If you decide to keep your feelings to yourself and not explore them, it is said you are "true to your partner." But are you being true to yourself? By hiding away your feelings you will feel sad or frustrated. Those kinds of feelings won't improve the relationship you are having with your partner.

You can also secretly have an affair. That would put a huge secret between you and your partner. Again, you have to hide your feelings. You have to come up with excuses to be with your secret lover. If the truth comes out, your partner will feel terrible. It can cause your relationship to end.

When you decide to leave your partner, you will have your reasons for doing so. Your current relationship can be boring, maybe the sex is bad, you could be frustrated about some parts of your partner's character or you don't like the way your life is in general at the moment. The new connection seems exciting, sensational, breathtaking . . . What you forget is that the issues you have in your current relationship are one hundred percent your responsibility, meaning that the same issues come back when this new connection turns into a stable relationship. You will be in the exact same situation, not being fully content with the life you live.

In an open relationship, you can explore this new connection as much as you like. This new person can be a perfect match for you in some areas of your life. Maybe not in all the areas, but that is not important. Both of you can focus on these parts where the pieces of the puzzle exactly match. And when you're done exploring, you can go back home and find the stable place that is your long-term relationship.

You are not forced to choose between possible partners. Because you don't have to choose, you don't have to hide your feelings to yourself or to your partner. You can be open about your emotions and share them.

The difference between your long-term partner and other connections is that your long-term relationship is (ideally) built on a steady foundation of shared principles and values, creating a very strong foundation. You will find your areas of growth and areas of interest built upon this foundation. Your partner will share some of these fields, but s/he will also have his/her own focus points. Why would you expect your partner to be an exact copy of yourself? That would be quite boring ... For the parts where your partner doesn't match perfectly with you, you can invite new connections. These connections can be very deep and even last a long time, but they will never replace the foundation you have built with your partner.

You also don't need to worry when a new connection doesn't exactly match your values, but you do feel very attracted to them. You could just explore the areas you are curious about, and let go afterwards.

And what if a new connection *does* match better in all ways? What if this foundation of principles and values is stronger than what you have built with your current partner? Well, that could be a sign it's time for you to move on...

The "danger" of finding a better match for you is independent of the type of relationship you have. Unless you are totally closed to meeting new people, there is always and everywhere a chance you will meet someone you like better than your current partner. In a monogamous relationship you always have to choose. Choose between your current partner and the new, exciting connection. Choose between your own feelings and the feelings of your partner. There is no option where everybody is happy.

In an open relationship you have the possibility to explore what attracts you so much in this new person. What lessons can you learn? What will this connection bring you *and* your long-term relationship? You can have a great time exploring and return to a safe haven where your partner is waiting for you with open arms.

Two baskets

Dr. Anya

It is
simple

A vast array of flowers
in a field beyond your vision

roses, poppies, daisies, sunflowers...

like waves of the sea, rising
and falling
in the wind

The sky blue, the morning just beginning
A basket
in each hand

The art of falling in love

Kala Pierson

I think it's no accident that so many historical examples of ethical non-monogamy involved artists, writers, and musicians. Sure, this freedom came partly from the license artists already have for living outside cultural norms. But more broadly, being a working artist means continually falling in love—with the things you're creating, with abstract concepts, with others' ideas and your own ideas, with surprises and fortunate detours. Creative fertility depends on fluidity. And the freedom to keep falling in love, not just with new ideas and projects but also with new minds and bodies, is a core part of my life.

I'm a classical composer who's been out as poly for seventeen years, since age twenty. For most of those years I was essentially solo-poly, involved in a beautiful weave of long-term and short-term relationships but living on my own in New York. Now I'm living in an open triad marriage based in Philadelphia. My wife, my husband, and I have been raising our preschooler, Noah, as three equal parents since he was born. The three of us had our formal wedding ceremony when Noah was sixteen months old, and he stole the show as only a toddler in a tiny tux can. (Later, for practical reasons, one pair of us also filed for a legal marriage license; the married-on-paper pair is different from the bio-parent pair, partly in order to establish more legal connection to Noah among all of us.)

Each of us also has other long-term, usually long-distance relationships outside our triad; mine range in length up to sixteen years. Of my other relationships, the most emotionally and creatively central is with a person who can't be at all out as poly. This has been hard for me in many ways, but in seven years of loving him, I've come to accept and understand the complexities of the closet. I have great empathy for those who can't safely be out yet.

My triad has the luxury of being entirely out, with approval from each of our families, safe work contexts, and no negative reactions from people in our son's life such as his teachers or classmates (aside from one girl's dismay at such an unfair distribution of resources: "Why does Noah get two moms? I want two moms!"). His daycare and preschool have each been exemplary in their welcome, always making sure to include all of us in his craft projects (such as the Thanksgiving placemat he brought home with two mom turkeys and a dad turkey).

Our negative interactions with strangers have been few and far between. Only one real verbal attack; generally just persistent, intrusive questioning. Sometimes strangers become fixated on finding out which two of us are "the real parents," refusing to accept our response that all three of us are the parents. One memorable low point was our server in a restaurant insisting repeatedly, even after we'd asked her to stop, that Noah point to his "real" mother. Sometimes it can feel exhausting that we're automatically out as poly whenever we've got a little guy in tow calling us Mommy, Mama, and Daddy. But a core agreement for us is being this straightforward when strangers are asking about our family—as a model for Noah, for our own peace of mind, and as a contribution toward poly visibility and normalization in general.

For me, this is a fantastic family structure (and probably the only structure in which I ever would've wanted to become a parent). Three to one feels like an ideal ratio for raising a child while maintaining space for each adult's career and identity. My spouses don't work in the arts, but they recognize my career and dedication as equal to theirs in importance—and that's not something every artist can say, even those in traditional dyad relationships.

While the three of us have definitely experienced the broader personality conflicts one finds in any marriage, we've been almost entirely without poly-specific conflicts. This is partly because none of us feels much possessiveness or jealousy anyway, but also because each of us individually had more than a decade of poly experience by the time we decided to form our triad. This meant the most critical communication skills were second nature for each of us, as was our default of respecting each person's autonomy and equality. (As one example, we agreed from the beginning that we don't want to decide any debate with a simple "you're outnumbered" if two of us hold one opinion and the third holds a different opinion.)

Oddly, I don't know of any other pro classical musicians who are out as poly. (I did get some wonderful emails and messages from closeted colleagues I hadn't known about, among many other positive reactions from my colleagues after the *Philadelphia Inquirer* ran an article profiling my family in 2013.) The classical music world is still socially conservative in some ways; it's not always the safe space one might imagine. I hope I can be part of an evolution toward more safety, over the years, by being straightforwardly out and visible. Writing the Great American Queer Poly Opera wouldn't hurt either.

My family, my home

Rose McDonnell

Who would have guessed
That in my difference
One of the many things that sets me apart
Outcast
Weird
I would have found this hidden world
Existing beneath and alongside the day to day
Hiding in plain sight

A whole community of open hearts
More freely flowing love
Acceptance
Joy
Than I ever thought I'd encounter

Yet still with a face toward reality
And the hard work
And sweat
Needed to keep all of this together
A willingness to face the hardships
And the strength and competence to overcome

Surrounded by support like I've never known it
Ears to listen

And arms to hold
From every direction
Friendship
Affection
Teamwork

Growing bonds stronger and more flexible than I knew
    to be possible
Weaving my heartstrings into this network
Astounded
Brought to tears
That the love I always dreamed of
Might be possible
Or even
Not ambitious enough
To account for what life seems to be building in my soul
And in those around me

Who would have guessed
After all the heartbreak
Rejection
And struggle
That I could finally find a place
A place that shows me the meaning of the words
Home
Family

It is almost too much to hope for
Yet something tells me we've only just begun

5/21/14

My rainbow

Michón Neal

There's a rather hilarious *Foster's Home for Imaginary Friends* episode that features a character named Cheese. Cheese proceeds to drive the other imaginary friends insane with his eccentricities. The Foster family is already a bit crazy to begin with, but Cheese stands out even more. At one point he dons women's clothes and declares that he and Bloo, another imaginary friend, are "brother ladies." I'm a bit like Cheese; I am the strangest person I know. You may need to search for some of these terms, but in addition to being a poor, female-bodied person of color, I am also a polyamorous, relationship anarchist, demisexual, rape survivor, pansexual, atheist, genderqueer, differently abled, sapiosexual writer of queer and poly fiction. These descriptors didn't cause one another and they are only aspects that happen to coexist in me. They may inform my choices, but they do not dictate them.

But I'm not here to define myself. I'm here to tell you about the family that helped define my life.

It starts with the person who's been in my life the longest: my sister. In a play on the term "brother ladies," my older sister and I affectionately call one another "brother mothers." In so many ways she has been my primary companion in life. We are fiercely devoted to one another, we are the best of friends, and we even raise our children together. We've lived together at various points in our lives and our goal is to one day all live together again. At first this dynamic can seem a bit strange to newcomers. My sister and I often jokingly call each other husband and wife. She was the breadwinner and mother figure and I was the father figure and caretaker for our children.

There's nothing incestuous about the relationship despite our teasing (we both share a rather sick sense of humor, as our friends can attest to). We've simply found that we naturally tend to place one another as number one. This is due in part to the way we grew up, where our lives literally depended on one another. Time and again we've proven ourselves devoted and trustworthy to one another, a very rare occurrence in our dealings with other people. We scope out one another's potential partners to determine if they're cool enough to be inducted into the Neal family. We know that no matter what else happens and no matter who enters or exits our lives that we are together forever.

From that solid base, we've built a foundation for the next generation of Neals. They learn from our example that romance, sex, and traditional forms of partnerships do not have to be the only form of love that is meaningful or important in their lives. I myself am a relationship anarchist; people don't earn a place in my life by default, we build a unique relationship based on our natural inclinations, desires, and compatibility. I take nothing in my life for granted or for given. I appreciate honesty, openness, and wisdom above all else. My friends and lovers came from all walks of life but those traits ran through all of them. My loved ones are a rainbow of diverse and wonderful people: I don't care about gender, sexuality, or the physical package as long as it is beautiful and contains a mind of gold.

My current long-term partner and I have spent nearly nine years together. He passed my sister's "test," even though it took him about three years to do so. He knows how important my family is to me, he's eager to learn, and he has taught me so much about true intimacy. We've only yelled at one another a few times. Literally, I can count on my hand the number of times either of us has raised our voice to the other. We're both great communicators and very early on we established a field of interaction based on transparency, practiced the "heard and understood" method for communicating our opposing views, and owning our shit. I've had experiences with him that are so bizarre, so elevated, and at times so incredibly painful that they almost seem like tales from my fictional world, the cuilverse.

I told him nearly as soon as I met him that I would not be chained, that I had a traumatic past, and that I would be the weirdest person he'd ever met. My upfront honesty paid off because he's still around. Though longevity doesn't always equal quality, I appreciate the fact that we were able to transition through so many periods in our lives together. At first he had to get used to the fact that my characters were as real to me as breathing people. He learned to share my time and energy with my characters and it helped him to accept the real-life lovers I later had.

He comforted me when two women I dearly loved, one of whom who had a sexual relationship with him as well, decided that they wanted to be monogamous with their boyfriends (I seem to have a very odd and specific track record with women; they all run off to marry men!). He listened to me when one of my former boyfriends called me a diseased whore. He went to the funeral in my stead when my other long-term boyfriend passed away from natural causes. That loss created a star in the heavens for me to look upon. The lover who left through death challenged my mind in ways I'd never thought possible. In every conversation we were peeling away layers of the world to discover what lay beneath. He was truly my star in so many ways. Yet it was short-lived; he supernova'd before his shine could reach the rest of the world.

My current long-term partner is about three thousand miles away right now, working and caring for our child along with my sister. They are holding down the fort while, for the first time in my life, I make my dreams a reality. Most of my dearest friends are there, too. There's the gay man who calls me his mistress and for whatever reason has me approve every man he dates. He's been in my life for nearly twelve years. I had once been in love with him (I seem to have a track record for falling in love with gay men as well). Painful though it was when he was finally brave enough to come out, and simultaneously break my heart, our friendship was able to survive and flourish. I inspired him to start writing and it's the most brilliant thing I've ever seen.

There's my creative soulmate, who I never have to explain an idea to. She and I talk a lot like my siblings and I do: in half-sentences, movie quotes, and exclamations that no one else would realize communicate paragraphs of descriptions and ideas. When it comes to our creative projects or the way our minds work, we sync up in a rather uncanny way. If my books are ever turned into movies, I can trust that she will make sure the designs and characters are exactly as I designed them. She understands my process in a way that no one else does and one day soon we might create a new story together.

There is one person in my life who I definitely cannot place in a box. There is no way to describe the relationship I have with the unrelated person I've known the longest. We attended two schools together when younger and now as adults have reconnected in the strangest way. It's a WTF-friendship, for sure. We can't figure out what it is we mean to each other; there's no term for it but we know that it's powerful and amazing. We see one another only a few times a year and yet each time is like the first time. He's the only person I know that I feel comfortable talking on the phone with (I detest talking on the phone). We never run out of topics to discuss. It always feels like our minds are touching when we're around each other or talking. Perhaps we simply resonate and that's what we feel. We can be delightfully awkward together and yet it's the most fun we've ever had.

I tell them all about the big house I hope we one day share (everyone with their own space, of course. Perhaps taking over an apartment complex would be ideal). We all miss one another terribly. The distance doesn't diminish the love we have for one another; it spurs us on to make the most of each beautiful and fleeting moment. Our family shape is flexible and ever-changing, with love as the bond that sets the rules for how it moves and morphs. I could not ever have this sort of intimacy, joy, and growth without being the queer and free weirdo that I am. There are so many facets of a person and it's difficult to discover them or your own when you lock yourself inside while it's raining outside. Take an umbrella if you need to but don't fear getting wet. Because you just might miss your rainbow.

I carry with me the treasure of the time I had with my now-deceased lover, bringing it with me through every part of my life. Though everything changes, my love never dies. The passion, beauty, and understanding I share with these people create the rainbow after the storm that was my life before. There are no guarantees, nothing is promised, and life is full of horrible surprises. Yet all of my loves' colors spread over the entirety of my life and nothing can take that away.

Monosaturated

Jessica Burde

I walk a road unknown, hand in hand with the one who walks beside me. My other hand swings freely in the dark. I long to join that hand with someone else's. To walk hand in hand as our roads run together.

But I (and my partner) have needed our free hands: to push aside branches or clamber over boulders. The few who touched my hand moved on, unable or unwilling to walk with me while I navigate these obstacles.

One day my path will smooth and my hand will clasp another without distraction. Or someone will join hands with me, and they and I (and my partner, as he chooses) will help each other through the obstacles that face us. Or perhaps my partner will find someone to hold his other hand, to navigate their obstacles together (and I with them).

Until that day comes I (we) are

Monosaturated

Tightening

Lina

Our family—not that to which we were born, but that which we have created—is a Chinese finger trap. You know those cylinders, woven together, that you put a finger in each end and pull? That's us. The harder you pull in opposite directions, the more effort you exert to tear it apart, the tighter it becomes. The fibers interweave ever more strongly, holding closer together, becoming more solid.

When the second person I ever loved became my wife, four years ago, we gave finger traps as one of the favors. There wasn't a philosophical reason behind them; they just made us smile and didn't cost too much. Ever since, when I see them, they remind me of our bond—an artifact stumbled across, a trinket imbued with meaning.

Growing up, I was taught that marriage was between a man, a woman, and God. "A three-stranded cord is not easily broken." I exchanged the man for a woman, and we let the mandatory third strand slip away as we fell in love with each other and our new reality. Two strands can be strong, too.

And yet, here I sit, with the family I have created: a three-stranded cord, a braided Chinese finger trap. Not by reintroducing a deity, but by the miraculous interweaving of fate that brought my first love back into my life; a spark, a flame, and the interlocking of his life with ours to create our triad, our perfect union, our family. Serendipity as reality.

Of course, we are not a dime a dozen, not like the way you find finger traps in novelty shops. And this woven bond of ours has taken more effort than the intertwining of colored wood or plastic. We have been tested, with great forces trying to pull us apart; we have buckled down, laced together, in the face of opposition.

And yet—opposition is not the only response. There are those who will sit and marvel with us at what wonders nature has wrought. "It's lucky enough to find one to love; how could I be upset with you for finding two?"

I understand. I, too, thought it impossible. I thought the obstacles insurmountable. But time has taught that by weaving together we can endure.

Pull, world. Pull against us. And as simple as a child's toy, we will cling to each other and know that therein lies our salvation.

Try the new compersion:
Jealousy be gone!
Phyllis-Serene Rawley

Tired of those nagging jealous emotions you can't seem to shed? Ready for a new emotion? Then try the new and improved emotional response called "compersion." It's so new it's not even in the Internet dictionary yet.

So why am I jealous? As a Leatherwoman, I practice and teach adults to explore their kink, fetish, or other expressions of expanded sexuality. But that green monster can ruin a hot dungeon scene.

Jealousy has caused many of my relationships to crash and burn. I don't know when love changes to possessiveness, but it does. After one ex-boyfriend decided to date my roommate, my response moved into violent attack mode. Thank goodness the internal rage also temporarily blinded me, so I saw red, and I was frozen. That gave me time to think, calm down, walk away, and find a new place to live.

I would prefer another emotion than the one that beats up my heart and mind like a bronchitis attack. Jealousy has a way of kidnapping my time and energy in directions I don't want to go. I recall the rush of unpleasant emotions that made my stomach knot up, my hand form a fist, words spew forth I would regret—all part of the cycle I wanted to break. But how could I break free of the green stain?

With the divorce rate in America comfortably above fifty percent, partnering for life is no longer the norm. I needed another emotion that could keep up with our societal change. At a polyamory meetup, I was introduced to the word: *compersion*, the antithesis to jealousy. Here's the Wikipedia entry on compersion:

> *Compersion is a state of empathetic happiness and joy experienced when an individual's current or former romantic partner experiences happiness and joy through an outside source, including, but not limited to, another romantic interest. This can be experienced as any form of erotic or emotional empathy, depending on the person experiencing the emotion.*

Nice concept, but the million-dollar question is, how can I be happy when MY old lover is loving someone else? Then I remembered the C.S. Lewis book, *The Four Types of Love*. Lewis defined the following types of love: agape, philia, eros, and storge.

Agape is the spiritual love you have that comes from your beliefs.

Philia is the bond of friendship.

Eros is the emotional intimacy we share in a relationship. (Venus is described as the "Fifth Love" and is the passion and energy of sexual exchange, its trademark being a temporary state of experience, like orgasm and infatuation.)

There is another, more powerful love that helps to explain the ability to convert jealousy into compersion.

Storge is the familial love of parent to child. Storge can be more powerful than all the others combined. It's the type of love that gives a parent superhuman strength to lift a car to save a child's life.

Compersion suggests that if we can adjust our thinking, heal our emotions, we can celebrate our partner's, lover's, spouse's, or ex's happiness in another relationship. We can replace jealousy with joy.

You also receive extra feelings of contentment and maturity with every use of compersion. Like when your child goes off to school for the first time or the last time, (hopefully) away to college. There is pride in being a part of making that success happen. And I like being a part of someone's success.

Jealousy can hold me in this knee-jerk reaction of anger, hurt, and then retribution. By reminding myself that the experience has passed, I can change my thoughts. If that doesn't work, then I remember why the relationship needed to end in the first place and my head clears, and I can look for the good of this new coupling and let the joy of compersion build in me.

Now have I done it? Not every time, but I'm working on it. It's not like one day you wake up compersed. It's the *art of letting go* of past anger that takes time and practice. And when I have a surge of emotions that race up to my brain and fist at the same time, I acknowledge the emotion and look at it. I then look at where I want my emotions to be and go there. No need to replay the old tapes. My heart calms, pulse slows, teeth unclench, and I can think without anger. I take a deep breath, let compersion in, and make a choice to celebrate my (ex) lover's new relationship and wish them well. It's that simple and that difficult. But the end result is my joy and happiness, and I'm definitely worth the effort.

The fourth story

Athena Affan

For some folks polyamory acknowledges something they've known their whole life—an inevitable destination for a natural inclination. For the three of us, my two live-in partners and I, we were monogamous until the day that we weren't. Polyamory happened to them through relationships with me, and for me, I only truly understood it when I fell hard for a girl. I'm a queer-identified woman of colour living on the unceded traditional territories of the Musqueam, Squamish and Tsleil-Waututh peoples, also known as Vancouver, BC, Canada. If you had told a younger me what my life would look like balanced on the precipice of age forty, she wouldn't believe you. How could I have possibly imagined that I would have a girlfriend and two live-in partners, and be one of three dedicated parents to a beautiful little boy? My story comes first I suppose but in the grand scheme of things it's just one page of many in the complex narrative of my poly family.

My dating history up until that point had been predictably and prize-winningly monogamous. My first boyfriend and I were together for a year. I was with the second for six months and the third for three years. Those early dating years were emotionally uncomplicated with each relationship beginning and ending without overlap. Even the infidelity of the third relationship felt simple; I was all but finished with that partner and had no desire to begin anything meaningful with the lover. The shift began about three years into my relationship with my fourth partner, Niall.

Niall and I were both struggling when we met: I was in recovery from an abusive relationship while he was fighting underemployment and depression. As a result our story originates in comfort and intention rather than passion. We moved in together after only a month of dating, rapidly finding safety and support in each other. He is a brilliant, introverted man who often manages to exist, in a child-like fashion, purely in the moment. I, on the other hand, am extremely extroverted: mind racing from topic to topic incessantly. A match made in heaven, right? Despite the inescapable personality conflicts that have plagued us throughout our relationship, we have found ways to weather these conflicts and continue moving forward together.

We had recently opened our relationship so I could participate in casual, lighthearted intimacy that was commonplace in one of my social circles at the time. During our negotiations I learned that Niall really didn't think about me much when I was out. "Don't you miss me or wonder what I'm up to?" I insisted, socialized to believe that jealousy equals love. He shrugged. "Not really. When you're gone I'm distracted by whatever I'm doing. Why would I think of you?" Okay, I'll admit that I was a little offended by this, but over the years I've come to realize it's just his nature. This quality has made it easy for us to navigate multi-partnered relationships. It's a perspective that has spared us from the tension of working through jealousy and helped us to be successful as a couple and as a family. When I felt the pull of exploring my bisexuality and appealed to him to open our relationship further, he was supportive and agreed.

I knew I was looking for something a little more in-depth with a woman than I had experienced previously, but I was pretty sure that that just meant sex. What else could it mean? So I met a sexy and wonderful woman, Christiane, and we totally had sex. To my surprise that was the least of it. We went to movies and out for meals. We watched TV, snuggled and talked. I felt this wonderful frisson when I was with her or thought of her and it finally hit me, we weren't sleeping together, we were dating! Not only that, I was falling for her. This experience was the starting point of my poly journey. I remember all of it so clearly: the deepening crush I had on her while feeling the same, perhaps even more committed to Niall. I had never dreamed or imagined that such a thing could be possible and yet loving two people was not the most remarkable part. What amazed me was how easily these feelings settled within me without inner conflict or strife. They just felt right.

Although Christiane and I had lots of fun together our relationship didn't last. In her wake I eagerly sought as many opportunities to flex this new many-loves muscle as possible. For better or for worse (usually for worse) I've discovered that I love falling in love. So like a bull in a china shop I crashed my way through a series of intense online romances that all ended in tears, typically mine.

Throughout these tragic pairings Niall was patient and tremendously supportive. In exchange, I made sure to keep him apprised during my endeavours. He was the first to know when I was getting to know someone, when I started crushing, and when I thought I might be falling in love.

In hindsight I didn't really know what I was looking for or have a particular destination in mind with these connections. Maybe I envisioned another lighthearted and fun dating relationship or passionate emails and phone calls at a distance. Maybe even a little bit of naughty Skyping. Amidst all of the cautious step-by-stepping through polyamory-in-practice I never really stopped to consider the entire scope of possibilities for myself or the future.

About seven years into our relationship, challenges arose. We both had recently experienced job loss in the wake of 9/11. We both were struggling with depression. I got it into my head that after this much time we should be more like a "real" married couple. Nothing Niall did was right. He was a terrible husband and I had no desire to be a wife. These judgements created an awful contradiction that led me to question why we were even together at all. All I could see were his flaws, and I was convinced that his thoughts were the same about me. It was the darkest time of our relationship and brought out the worst in both of us. We found temporary solace and a little bit of connection with one another in the form of a multiplayer online role-playing game. It was into that context that Patrick entered our lives.

Patrick was a friend of a friend in the game and acquaintances of both Niall and me. I was angry at life, bitter at home and jaded about online relationships so I initially rebuked his good-natured attempts at befriending me. When I relented and began to get to know him it turned out that his light, down-to-earth conversation was just what I needed. Even though speaking with him was so easy and natural I think we were both caught off guard when we allowed ourselves to acknowledge the depth of our growing attraction and intensifying feelings. The problem with this situation? He lived in Minneapolis, MN, more than fifteen hundred miles away.

Our story is a journey from distance to connection and the point at which things really became interesting for all of us. Once Patrick and I started we couldn't look back. Neither of us stopped to ask where we were going. Neither of us considered the future because it was just too scary to contemplate. What future could there be for us with me in an established partnership with Niall an entire country and many miles away? At some point, particularly when doubt edged its way into the scene, one of us would gently remind the other, "Let's just take it day by day." This mantra kept us hopeful and sane as we agreed to follow our path no matter where it led. As silly as it may sound, we truly let our hearts guide us and decided to meet in Minnesota that fall, then again early the next year. By summertime, less than a year after we met, he had moved to Seattle, WA, a mere four hours' drive away.

Over the next four years of our long-distance relationship Patrick and I established ourselves as a couple. Jealousy came between us on several occasions and we were constantly engaged in a battle of time and distance. As Patrick and I became more serious the relationship structure between the three of us crystallized as well. In the beginning Patrick often tried dismiss his needs by saying that he was "just the secondary." I think it made it easier for him to cope with our situation but for me it was like an intimacy-proof wall between us. I am both Niall's and Patrick's only partner: their main person! How could I put one of them ahead of the other emotionally? I couldn't. A non-hierarchical structure in which both of them were just partners, rather than primaries or secondaries, just made sense for us. It certainly went a long way toward allowing my relationship with Patrick to shift, flex and eventually grow into the mature relationship it would one day become.

Falling in love with Patrick changed my life. His unconditional love for me reminded me how to love unconditionally in return. In that open, vulnerable headspace I was able to gain some significant insights about Niall and me. I could once again see his strengths as well as his flaws and I realized that I was so caught up in an idea of who we should be that I had forgotten who we were. Most importantly I could see that there was something valuable between us that had kept us together for so long. He had always been there for me, and despite how difficult things were, Patrick and I would not be possible without Niall's ongoing, genuine support. With renewed but tentative hope in one another Niall and I dedicated time, effort, and yes, lots of individual and couples therapy towards resolving our issues. We embraced change, grew as individuals and finally made our way towards loving each other more deeply than ever before.

In our tenth year Niall and I bought a home together and Patrick moved in with us. We took this terrifying, life-changing step with goodwill and have persevered through dedication and hard work. It has been neither perfect nor easy. We operate like two couples sharing a household, their relationship resembling that of friendly (most of the time) roommates. This comes with many challenges and lack of communication abounds. When disagreements arise I'm often caught in the middle as both of them prefer to engage with me rather than each other. Still there have been times I've seen them so upset with each other one day to just put it aside and behave normally the next day. As an extrovert this kind of non-communication drives me absolutely nuts; however, when I look at this in a different light, their behaviour is actually very mature. They regulate their emotions and try to keep our home comfortable. I'd like to think this is for my sake but I think it's more about commitment to an unspoken agreement we share about what family, at least our little family, is about: acceptance, keeping the peace, compromise, patience and yes, love. I cannot think of two men with a greater dedication to family even though I think we've only recently, tentatively, began to think of ourselves as such.

So we finally arrive at the present. The page opens on a typical moment for us today: Patrick lies on the sofa in our living room while I sit on the floor beside him. We both watch as Niall plays with our son, Nate, born one short year ago. Niall and I have been together for seventeen years now, and Patrick and I for eleven. We have all been living together for seven years. Three years ago we embarked on a new adventure: parenthood. The idea took shape through several gentle and cautious conversations about their dreams of fatherhood and my dream of two children, one with each of them: the most important individuals in my life.

There have been some logistics: a complicated discussion about who would be the first biological father, how to coordinate three different personalities and parenting styles and the decision to come out to all of our families. Niall's family is local while Patrick's is in the US. When we contemplated a family unit consisting of two babies with two different dads, we knew that we wanted siblings to be accepted and treated equally by family. So we came up with the idea of keeping Nate's biological parentage private as we shared my pregnancy, our baby's "dad squared" status and our poly reality. For the curious, Niall and Patrick share a similar physical description; nah, I don't have a type.

That was just the beginning because what followed were the trials and tribulations of pregnancy and birth: trying to conceive and then facing loss due to miscarriage, supporting the non-biological father to take ownership of his role as an equal parent while making sure that the biological dad felt secure with sharing his genetic "thunder," managing family hostility after coming out, blazing trails at the hospital with our midwife advocating for both fathers to be in the delivery room during the birth, and constantly learning and relearning how to rally together in support of our son. Despite what feels like an impossible learning curve our little boy is fiercely loved. It's a delight to watch him reach for hugs from each of us in turn after a scare or a hurt—he knows exactly who his parents are.

When I reflect on the previous chapters of our lives it's hard to believe that we've come this far. The scariest part is that we've been flying by the seat of our pants the entire time. There are no rules or instruction manuals about how to do what we're doing and yet, impossibly, it's working. I look at our wonderful little boy and see a physical manifestation of our love, hopes, dreams and even fears. I see the culmination of our efforts and the concrete evidence of our communal growth. Like a good book Nate's story was the plot twist that none of us saw coming. Just one thing remains: will there be another baby? I'll admit to having a little bit of doubt. After all, Nate soaks up all the love we have and more; how will we possibly love another child as much? In eager anticipation I guess we'll just have to wait and see.

Part III: At the kids' table

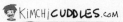

A bigger boat

Ann

I am not one of the world's best long-term planners, which ends up being both an asset and a liability. Children with my husband, Chris, was always a part of my very vague plan, but a poly family was a bit of a surprise. And while parenting under the most mundane of circumstances involves a great deal of making it up as you go along, this is doubly (or triply or quadruply, etc.) true of poly families with children. And while we have a great many poly friends, nobody had experiences that would provide any kind of road map for us. So, we continued to make it up.

Who has which responsibilities? Certainly the buck stops with the biological parents (though I'm sure there are some families out there where this is not the case), right? Who is considered part of the family, and what does that mean? As our partners' lives and ours become more closely knitted together, the interfaces between our partners and the children become increasingly complex. I mentally scouted around for other models: stepparents? Not quite the same. There's no element of one parent being replaced with another who will either suffer or excel by comparison; both original parents are still there. Significant other of divorced parent? That's a little bit closer—but again, the child has not lost the consistent presence of one parent, nor the dynamic between them. There are certainly plenty of poly families who maintain greater separation between the children and their parents' partner(s) or lover(s), but that's not what ended up happening in our family, and the dynamic that has grown up is a lovely one, though even establishing terminology is challenging. Will came up with "trans-parent"; I have heard "social parent" used as well. That gets into the issue of what the word "parent" even entails—is it a term reserved for relationships defined by biology or marriage? And as with virtually everything else where poly is concerned, the answers to all of these questions are entirely subjective and the structures of the families are all unique.

One thing became immediately obvious: the logistical advantages to a family with four adults and two children are countless. There are now many available combinations and permutations for "good cop/bad cop" strategies. It is amazing to see an issue that becomes a battle-to-the-death with Chris or me is more easily defused by our partners. Meredith is a staunch enforcer of vegetable consumption at dinnertime, and Will has a lovely knack for detecting mischief being perpetrated by my youngest. Where one person gets stuck, another person can come up with the necessary and often inexplicable alchemy needed to resolve some sort of child-crisis. Trips require more planning, but the execution of them is a whole new world when you've got four adults shepherding two children.

The oft-voiced reassurances within the poly community, that love is not a limited resource, and in fact begets more love, have rung entirely true for me with respect to my children. When my eldest went to sleepover camp for the first time, she wanted a picture of her family in case she got homesick—all six of us. I do not feel like less of a mother when the kids want Meredith to tuck them into bed, or when our partners are added to stick-figure drawings of the family. It is honestly heartwarming, and I feel pleased and relieved that they feel surrounded by a greater-than-usual number of adults who love them, and whom they can trust. Will has been a presence in my youngest child's life since the very beginning of it—he was on the receiving end of countless savage nighttime kicks while she still occupied my body. There is a much higher level of trust and commitment needed when children are involved; regardless of the level of responsibility or inter-action on the part of the parent(s)' partner(s), the children do not exist in a vacuum. Frankly, it can be terrifying. But the experience of being in the midst of the abundance of love in a poly family that embraces children…it is almost impossible to describe. There don't seem to be any maps for the road that we're on, but our hearts seem to be carrying us in the right direction.

We have a running joke in our family—that the kids are not allowed to do anything fun or dangerous until they are thirty-five (date, drive, go to concerts, etc. We're mostly kidding. Mostly.). Upon my husband's reminder that I would turn thirty-five next year, I gleefully said that I would finally be old enough to do all of these forbidden things. My eldest looked at me, rolled her eyes and said, "Mom. You ALREADY have a boyfriend."

Fractals of love

Rev. Claudia Hall

Writing this reflection on being a poly family has been surprisingly hard. One of the things I ask myself a lot is what makes a family. For myself, as a minister and as a poly person, I see love and covenant at the heart of family. Not just romantic or sexual love, but the kind of deep commitment to stay together through the good and the bad. Important note here, I am not talking about enduring abuse, but about a covenant that is mutual and dedicated to helping one another through the difficult times. So an *active* love that seeks the best possible outcome—for self, for others, and for the world—is what I hold to be the foundation for healthy families. Beyond that core, each family is different.

My family doesn't fit a neat chart or tree, rather it is a fractal image both chaotic and orderly. At the core of it all is my adorable son, who has multiple disabilities and requires around-the-clock care. A lot of families go through divorce when they have a child like this, and I know why. All that you have goes to the baby, and there is nothing left for relationships. Here is where having three parents is good, there is always a built-in babysitter. Here is also where multiple relationships is hard, because in addition to the exhaustion of raising a special needs child, we also juggle lots of relationships at different levels.

In our case, "family" looks like a wife and two husbands raising a special needs child. Before that it looked like a military family where one member was deployed. Since our son was born, I have been diagnosed with a chronic immune problem which makes every day an additional challenge. In each case, we have faced these problems together because that is what we agreed to do. Active love at work. Active love making a family extends beyond my home as well. We have a network of aunts and uncles for our kiddo. Only a few share DNA with him, but all have committed to assist us in caring for and raising this special person. They are the next arc of the family constellation. Some live close and we see them often, others live at varying distances, but thanks to the technology of today they are present to support us on Facebook, through texts and calls, and so on.

Spiraling out even more, we come to the caregivers who provide services for my son. Doctors, nurses, therapists, teachers, social workers, and case managers, the list goes on and on. Yes, caring for my son is their job. They get paid for it, and they see lots of kids like mine every day. Yet each and every one of them chose to go into pediatrics, chose to work in programs and clinics known for focusing on the most disadvantaged children. They too are part of the family, distant arcs to be sure, but without their active love and care my son would not be alive. Their commitment to their professions has gifted our lives, and I owe them a debt of thanks.

Spiral back in and down, narrowing and deepening our view of the fractal, we return from love-as-caregiving to love-as-*eros*, the combined romantic and sexual intensity that brings people together and which often marks poly as different from intense friendships. For me the depth of emotional connection is the key difference between partners and friends, although sexuality plays a large role. No matter how connected I am to my friends, I don't have sex with them. While I am poly, my two husbands are both monogamy oriented, and our agreement is that if any of us meets someone else we will talk it through, as our core commitment is to our son and each other over all others.

This agreement was challenged recently when I met an amazing triad who lived out of state. We clicked right away and I began dating all three of them. My life was already insanely busy, so there have been a lot of bumps in the road, but things are going well as we offer each other not only romance, but a stabilizing influence outside the core relationships.

My out-of-state trio also has a minister in it, although he and I serve different denominations and in different ways, he as a chaplain and I as a community minister. He and I know that we would not be good as a full-time couple, since we can't seem to leave the job at work very well and we bleed into each other if we aren't careful. But we are very happy being each other's "backup," and our spouses are happy we have someone else to yammer on to about the subtle nuances between process theology and Universalist theology. So as ministers, and lovers, it works for us. As a person juggling multiple romantic partnerships it is a challenge, but it works. All of us see the gift in this, whether we claim it from God or Goddess or Providence or Fate (we have five faiths among the six of us). As a person of faith, the expansion of love is important to me, representing my attempt to live deeper into my faith each day.

Some poly folk I know have experienced negativity and hate from the church when they came out, and I have had my share of negative experiences with oppressive leaders in churches. Yet I have remained in my faith because I have found a theology that works, allowing me to integrate my religion-of-origin with my identity as poly. For me it was as simple as the fact that God is love. True *agape* love is unconditional, an ideal I have yet to achieve. But I have learned to love many people, some with a simple human compassion, some as friends, and some as partners and lovers. The core of my faith is very simple: God is love, so the more we love the more we participate in God. Among human beings, we learn to love through our relationships with others, so my relationships are expressions of my spiritual life.

I want to be clear that I feel we are all called into relationships in different ways. For some it may be singleness, for some monogamy, for some kids, for others none. There is not a right or wrong amount of people, just a right or wrong for you. For me, right this moment, the right amount is my son, my two husbands, and a trio I date. For every other family I know it looks different, but the good relationships all have this in common: they talk, they laugh, they respect each other, and they grow in love throughout the years.

I don't know what my family will look like in five years, or in twenty. I do know that there will be love and laughter, struggle and pain, joy and loss. I know that we will be just like everyone else and yet totally unique. I know that we will be committed to one another and to the love we share. In my world, this is what makes a family, everything else is just frosting on the cake.

These kids are all right

Nora

A couple of weeks ago while I was washing the dishes, my ninth grader walked into the kitchen and shoved his headphones onto my ears.

"What?" I asked, distracted.

"Song for you," he replied.

The song was Hozier's *Someone New*, which talks about how there's no right way to love, and how the singer falls in love with someone new every day.

Both my teenage sons reacted with admirable tolerance and maturity to my revelation, a few months ago, that my boyfriend has a wife and children. But because they're different people, each of my boys has developed his own unique perspective on polyamory.

The son with the headphones is the younger of the two. He's the junior team's starting quarterback, on the honor roll, at ease in any social group. His Instagram feed is full of beautiful girls, many of them with their arms around him, but he tells me he doesn't have a particular girlfriend. Too busy, apparently.

This son's reaction to my poly lifestyle and beliefs has been respectful and reflective. He's fine with whatever I do, he tells me. He can see that my partner loves me and treats me well, and that's what matters, he says. He has never expressed a personal opinion for or against poly-amory: this is a child who thinks for a long time before speaking his mind. But every now and then, I catch him thinking aloud—like with that Hozier song. A few weeks before that, he was talking to me about a favorite TV series, *Friday Night Lights*, in which a teenage love triangle endures for several seasons: two best friends, both appealing characters, are in love with the same girl. It's sad for all of them, he said. Sad that the girl has to choose. And then he looked at me, meaningfully, but said nothing more. Fourteen years old.

His brother is seventeen and a classic Taurus: large, blustering, tempestuous, stubbornly loyal. He is a homebody, devoted to family. At his elementary school they told me that there was often competition, amongst teachers, to get him onto a class list: "because when the biggest kid in a class is kind and gentle, bullies are less likely to emerge." Of my two kids, this one struggled harder with my divorce—he identifies closely with his dad, but is wired to return the love of anyone who loves him. He bonded quickly with his father's new girlfriend and his step-siblings, while learning to be the man of the house for me, his newly single mom. It took him a while to give up the impulse to take sides in the divorce, and to get comfortable with the idea that it can be okay when families change.

This son *does* have a girlfriend—his first. They're madly in love, as he'll gleefully tell anyone who will listen. "Polyamory may be okay for you, Mom," he says; "but it's not for me. I could never share my girl with anyone."

When his girlfriend is upset, he sits up with her all night on Skype, talking it out. He attends meetings of his school's gay/straight alliance because he likes helping people get along. He's considering majoring in human sexuality when he goes to university next year. He'd make a good counselor; warm and full of goodwill. He has an unshakeable belief in love.

Last month, my younger son played in the provincial football championship. In the stands cheering him on were his divorced parents, his brother, both his grand-mothers, his dad, his dad's girlfriend and the step-siblings on that side, me, my partner, my partner's wife and their son. We all sat together.

I think the kids'll be all right.

Parenting as a triad

K.H.

I'm a woman in my mid-thirties, and I'm one of three parents in a polyamorous family. We are a committed triad, and our life together as partners has never been separated from our life as parents. In fact, I can say confidently that the work of building our three-person relationship has prepared us better for parenthood, and that the challenges of parenthood have been met with more joy and confidence since we each have two other people to share them with.

J. and I had been together well over a decade and were married and functionally monogamous when we met E. We had looked for a third partner for many years with no success. We had one young son and were expecting our second. She was unmarried and had no children, and had never been in a poly relationship. He and I spent as much time together and with our son as we could, and so when we started dating E. our son was there to witness us getting to know each other. On our first three-person "date," the four of us accompanied J.'s parents to a summer festival and went to lunch at a diner. This may not be the usual way other poly triads start seeing each other, but that's what worked for us. You could say that even from the beginning, we experienced life as a family.

What started out as a deeply private experience as a triad and small family has gradually expanded as J. and I became more involved in E.'s everyday life and she with ours. I felt some trepidation when she began to tell friends that she was in a romantic relationship with a couple and not an otherwise single man. Frankly, I was worried that they would assume she was being exploited. Thank goodness, most of her friends allowed our behavior to speak for us, and her happiness proved far more important to them than whatever their initial reservations may have been.

When our second son was born, E. was there to support me at his birth. She held him and I watched with awe as she became a mother in front of my eyes. We didn't know anyone else personally in a situation like ours. Nevertheless, it felt natural to care for our boys together and it wasn't long before we were living together full time.

That was over three years ago. In the intervening time we have experienced the deaths of two of our parents, job changes, the completion of a master's degree, another move and two more births. E. became a biological mother last year, and I'm now in her position of mothering a child without having social recognition of the privilege or the effort. There have been challenges. There has been a tremendous amount of joy, and love. We're in it for the long haul. We know it, our kids know it, and our nearest and dearest do, too.

It took me about a year into our relationship as a triad before I managed the courage to tell my mom. She was remarkably sanguine about the whole thing, and I will always be grateful to her for how calmly she handled the news. My folks, who have been married for almost three decades now, have welcomed and loved E. as part of the family from that point on. They have been a wonderful example of acceptance, and I couldn't be more grateful for their support. My sister is gay and had at least one poly friend when we began our triad. She has loved and supported us the whole way. My parents have given me a lot of hope that people who are new to the concept of polyamory can adapt to polyamorous people in their lives and the newly flexible definitions of family relationships that this entails.

The decisions (because there are many tiny, incremental ones) that add up to how out we are as a poly family are still happening. It's a delicate balance. We weigh the benefits of owning our choices and respecting the people we care about by giving them the truth against the risks of being socially and professionally ostracized. It's true that living in the Bible Belt is hard if you're queer. It's harder if you're queer AND poly. Nevertheless, I have been impressed by how consistently open-minded friends and family members have been when dealing with our unusual family.

We still continue to exercise caution when opening up about our relationship to acquaintances and conservative family members. However, when E. gave birth our lives changed very much for the better. We can't really hide now, and I for one don't want to. I am not and never will be ashamed of our relationship. I won't allow myself for one moment to be ashamed, because even though relationships like ours are frequently vilified when they aren't publicly invisible, I'm certain that we aren't doing anything wrong by loving each other. I won't behave like I'm ashamed, either, because shame is a poison that would infect our kids' feelings about their family and therefore themselves. I think that behaving as if our family situation was something to hide would be worse for our children than anything other people could ever do to us.

The shape of our family, however inexplicable to those not in the know, is definite and real. I'd like to think that by our existence we're making a difference, however small, in how those who know us view the validity of unconventional relationships. I do know one thing, though—we're definitely making a difference in our kids' lives by giving them three parents' worth of attention and love.

Surprise! It's a polyfidelitous triad.

E.

This is not the life I anticipated for myself. But it's the life I stumbled upon. It's the life I've grown to recognize as ideal for me. It's the life I love.

We don't really think of ourselves using your typical poly labels, but if we did I suppose we'd say we're a polyfidelitous triad. Labels seem harsh and restrictive and prone to the fostering of assumptions, so I've never been much of a fan. Most of the time we just think of ourselves as a family. I know that my family is different from other families—especially in my geographical area. But really—as you hear from most poly families, I'm sure—we're really not all that different. We have four kids who we love and try our best to raise to be decent and interesting people, we go to the farmers market and go out for sushi and watch movies and dream about how to best decorate our house and best use our land, we talk and argue and forget and learn with each other, and we worry about money and try to eat well and wish we had more time to pursue all of our interests. I think we're pretty typical.

My partners of four years are a married couple who've been together for twenty years (since they were teenagers). They were looking for me—or some approximation of me—for years. And while I say I wasn't really looking for them, I was looking for the things they offer: stability, variety, longevity, love. Because they were established, there was a sort of security built in when I met them. I knew they were both good at commitment. I knew that if they said they'd stick it out, they could and would.

There was also a training ground built in. I knew that if I misunderstood one of them, the other would be there to help illuminate the situation with the kind of wisdom that comes from knowing someone for decades. I can watch him love her, and I learn how to better love her. I can watch her shrug off a word or an action that would have hurt me in the past, and I learn to not take him so seriously (and when to take him more seriously). For a person who was raised by a single mom and had no real example of a relationship to learn from, I can confidently say that being in a triad has helped me learn how to have any sort of relationship with another person at all. I still have a lot to learn, but if it weren't for this couple, I think I would still be years behind relationally.

As I said, even though I was not looking for them, my partners were looking for me. But I am not exactly what they expected either. They like color and I wear mostly black. They assume the best about people and about our future and I'm pretty anxious about everything. They're always genuine and forthright and I'm pretty snarky and ironic (so they say). They believe in sustainability and I always forget to put the vegetable scraps in the compost bucket. They are pretty touchy-feely and I like words better. They verge on hoarding and I like minimalism. They enjoy socialization and being with each other ALL

OF THE TIME, and I'm an introvert. I'm sure there are days when they look at me and wonder how in the world they ended up here with me. But we love each other and are committed to our little family, and we make each other laugh all of the time (sometimes at each other, but still). And we balance each other out pretty well... When you have three adults, there are much greater odds that someone will be good at something you're not so good at.

Which brings me to what is perhaps the biggest difference between my partners and me... They are very open and unafraid of being themselves and unapologetic about loving who and how they please, and I'm very private and am still frequently preoccupied with what other people think (although I usually say that I try to consider how my actions/lifestyle will impact others—which I think can be a gentle, loving way to be when it's not done out of fear).

The issue of whether and how to be "out" is the hardest part of my life, easily, right now. I know that if it were up to them, we'd shout it from the rooftops that we love each other. But, for me, it's more complicated. We live in a small town, one where I grew up and where my mom still lives. I love my mom dearly. She is a tough lady, but she is dealing with the death of my father and dealing with her issues of learning to live alone and aging. It pains me that my life—as much as I love it—would cause her any additional stress or sadness. It seriously pains me.

I told my mom about our relationship when I unexpectedly got pregnant. I didn't really have an option, because I knew that there was no way around the "Who's the father?!" question. It was the most difficult period in my life—particularly the period when I realized I had to tell her and was deciding how to tell her and then the six months after. It did not go very well at all. But the world did not end either! My mom still loves me and loves my baby, but she will not visit our house and does not want me to ever speak of my partners. I do my best to abide by her wishes and I try my best to straddle a line that is unpleasant for everyone involved. I try to be cheerful and see the silver linings; I try to keep everyone happy. I listen to my partners when they express their sadness and frustration over this situation, and I do my best not to feel like a failure or a phony. I wish I could make it all better, but I don't know how.

Even though the hardest part of being "out" is over—my mom, my brother, and the friends I've chosen to keep all know—the journey isn't over. I still worry about who else will find out, because I don't want my mom to be ridiculed or pitied. I don't want her to feel like she has to defend me. I don't want her to feel judged by my actions.

Another factor is that I am the primary breadwinner in our family and I work for a company that is extremely conservative. I do not think they would fire me over my lifestyle, but I do think people could make it a hostile environment for me. And I consider this in deciding who to be open with and how much to tell.

Not to mention that I just plain like my privacy. I don't really want to be a poster child for polyamory or have to be a vocal advocate for my choices. Honestly, I don't want to have the coming out talk with everyone I know. I just want to live my life like everyone else gets to. As time has gone on (especially since I've had a baby, which has sparked curiosity), I've become more "out" where it feels safe. I don't worry as much about people's assumptions as I did in the past. I would imagine that most of the people at our farmers market and at the local coffee shop have a basic assumption of what the dynamics are, but they don't usually ask and I don't feel compelled to lay it all out there. It is only a struggle when people I don't trust get too nosy, and my anxiety and desire to protect my family from rejection or hate gets the best of me. But I'm learning how to make this all work for me and for us, and for now I just take deep breaths and make one step at a time.

I know that as our children grow there will be more people who know the nature of our family. I don't want our kids to feel like they have to hide anything. I know we may encounter new concerns as they reach different stages in life, but I try not to think too far ahead. I think the best we can do is to love our children right here, right now, so we give them good attention, show them examples of healthy relationships, and teach them as much as we can. I think we are doing really well at this. We are pretty much the most stable, loving, rich family I know—not to brag. But it's true! I really stumbled into something totally beautiful and sweet and I'm proud to be a part of its ongoing creation and growth and revision.

My family

Maya Avery Combes

Conversations with my four-year-old son, Jax, about polyamory

By Christine and Jax

Me: Jax, what do you think about Mommy's friends?

Jax: You have lots of many friends!

Me: What different kinds of friends?

Jax: Some are like friends that are other mommies and some are like friends who come to our house and some are like special friends.

Me: Special friends?

Jax: Like Mr. David or Dr. Chris. Like the ones you like to kiss.

Me: Mmm hmm.

Jax: Because you like to have many special friends but some grown-ups like to just have one special friend, like Granny and Rumpah are just one special friend for each other.

Me: What do you think about that?

Jax: I think that they are happy.

Me: Mmm hmmm.

Jax: I like to have many friends but I don't like kissing so I don't have special friends.

Me: Do you think you will have one special friend or many when you grow up?

Jax: I will invent a special kissing machine to do that for me so I can have a house for a family of special friends but not have to kiss them.
Me: "Sounds like a plan."

EXPLAINING TO FRIENDS
"It means to be poly-Amish when you like to kiss lots of people and eat with them even when some people just choose one best friend for kissing. Then they get mono."

WHO IS THAT GUY?
"He's one of my mom's boyfriends. She has to have many doings of them because she has too many happy and sad and feelings to make my one Daddy too busy."

ROMANTI-KISS HOUSING
Jax: Why didn't Daddy choose to live at our house anymore? Does he want to live with Ms. Annie instead?
Me: Mommy and Daddy still love you very much, but our relationship with each other isn't romantic anymore and we weren't very good roommates.
Jax: So he got his own house?
Me: Yup.
Jax: And he doesn't wanna live with Ms. Annie?
Me: I don't know, but right now he's choosing a place by himself. He loves Ms. Annie romantically but that doesn't mean they will live together.
Jax: Oh. Kinda like you and Mr. David love each other in the romanti-kiss way, but you are too messy and he is very clean?
Me: Precisely!

Jax: So, when I am grown up I can choose who will be in my house and they don't have to romanti-kiss me"
Me: Yup, you don't have to be romantic with the people you live with, and the people you're romantic with don't have to live with you.
Jax: Good. I will choose to live with good cleaners so I don't have to do that and we won't be romanti-kissing unless we change our minds.
Me: Good plan!

My parents' polyamorous relationship, as viewed from ages fourteen and eighteen

Denali

When he was fourteen, Denali wrote the following post as a guest blog on his mother's website:

When I was young, I had no idea of what polyamory was. My parents just seemed like parents. All I knew was that my mom's boyfriend was practically part of the family. He was great with kids, and I would look forward to his visits. He was an influential adult in my early life. When I started to see the real picture, at about eight years old, it still seemed normal. The topic would occasionally come up around friends, and I got mixed reactions. The most common was: "That's weird." In fact, that was all I ever heard for years. Only in the past two years have I ever had a different reaction. There are two others: "That's wrong," and "That's awesome." All of my best friends today have said the latter. To this day, most of what it means to me is just more family friends. It has always been nice to have someone outside of the family visit, to go on a hike or have dinner with them.

Now to answer another question: are kids whose parents are poly likely to grow up to be poly themselves? I don't know. My parents haven't influenced my personal preference, but for all

I know, it's possible. It's not for everyone. The important thing though, is that it doesn't hurt anybody. For me, all it meant was more parental figures in my life, more fun adults whose company I would enjoy, and that is still the case. I see no reason to assume it will ever be any different. For some reason, the idea has never seemed personally appealing, and I think I've figured out why. The reason monogamy exists is partly because people can be too jealous to trust their partner to someone else. This often stems from poor self-esteem, the fear that someone else is better than you. Don't get me wrong, the fact that people sometimes just love one person is a huge part, but the jealousy factor is important too, and so often overlooked.

Were there any problems with this growing up? Not really. As I mentioned before, the only issue I ever had was when friends would look down on my parents. And again, these people always had so many other disagreements with me, disagreements about political, moral, and religious views, to name a few. Is there anything morally wrong with adultery? Yes, in my opinion, but adultery and polyamory are not the same thing. Polyamory requires an agreement from everyone involved. The real crime of adultery is the lying. By these definitions, no religion even so much as mentions polyamory, whereas adultery is generally not cool.

Also, my parents have one of the strongest relationships I've ever seen. They disagree occasionally, everyone does. But never, in fourteen years, have I received even the slightest hint that there was anything wrong with their marriage. Only once has there been a jealousy problem with any of the other relationships my parents were in with other people. Again, this is partly because they feel comfortable enough with their relationship that they feel no need for jealousy. Polyamory isn't my thing, but I see absolutely no reason why it can't work for other people, and fourteen years of exposure have not taught me otherwise.

Four years later, Denali is eighteen and reflects on his initial post for this book:

The only thing about my parents' decision to have an open marriage that annoyed me when I was younger was always how hard it was for me to explain to people. I would be trying to tell someone a story, and when I mentioned "my mom's boyfriend," I would see that look creep across their face. "Wait…" they would say slowly, as if they were unsure whether they were remembering right, "I thought your parents were married?" I hated answering this question. Not because I was ashamed of my parents, but because I felt like I was talking to a small child. "Of course they are," I would say, probably too sarcastically. "Their marriage just works differently."

As I grew up, I started to learn more about polyamory in general. Ever since I was around twelve or thirteen, it has seemed to me like a perfectly functional relationship dynamic, but until recently, I never thought it would work for me particularly. It's hard not to let jealousy get in the way. And I've known as many polyamorous relationships challenged by someone's inherently monogamous nature as vice versa. But in the past couple of years, I've come to feel a lot better about my relationships when it doesn't seem like someone is being treated like property by the other, which is why a polyamorous approach has been working for me recently. But if there's one thing I've learned from having both examples in my family, it's that what works for some people is not guaranteed to work for others. People just need to be honest about what they want.

Running for State
Kevin Glass

The subtle autumn chill pervaded the sculpted, suburban, grass hills of Woodward Park, the designated course of the California State Cross Country Championship. The wind carried with it the dreams and aspirations of many families from across California to the park on that day. The pressure should have been to a bursting point; however, in its stead was an eerie calm.

Sure, the competition was tough, but I had nothing to fear; the race itself was more of a reward for a successful season than anything else. Thankfully I had the fortunate position of relative mediocrity, free from the responsibility of being highly ranked.

If there was any stress from the meet, it was not due to the race itself, as I had run the course before. It was my family. The explanations and looks of disapproval, ostracization, and disruption of friendships were the bulk of what I was worried about. A polyamorous family isn't exactly the most socially acceptable background, given that even among liberal crowds it is a bit of a taboo.

Strolling up to the tent were my father, my mother, and my father's partner of seven years, with my two brothers following suit. My father's partner was holding his hand while my mom was talking delightedly with both of them, laughing about a familiar joke. This was the first time my entire family had been to one of my meets together and I was nervous. How would my teammates react? Would they judge me or ask why my mom hadn't divorced my dad yet, like other kids did?

It was nearer to my race, and our coach called for us to warm up. A quick glance at my teammates implied that they were a tad on the nervous side, but for different reasons. All the training, all the effort, all the missed hours after school—all of that was devoted to this moment, the time when we'd succeed at State. Each and every one of us had at that point gone through several pairs of running shoes, dashing up extremely steep hills, and running stretches greater than twelve miles at least once a week. Pushing and charging and stretching under ever darker sunsets, we were here. For me, being there was not about aspiring to a goal; it was accomplishment enough. Had someone told me two years prior that I would be running at State, I would have laughed. When I started the sport, I could not run farther than five miles in a stretch. I was forty-eighth on my team (of a team of fifty-two), and was not paid any attention to beyond being some sophomore in the back. Yet, I had a race to run, a race that was, at that point, the result of two years of self-reflection, improvement, and courage. It should have been a moment of intense giddiness, that I would finally have my reward for such a vast improvement.

However, as one would guess, the anxiety did not wear off when I started the warm-up. After going through the usual ritual, my group went back to the tent, doing various drills and putting on running flats in preparation for the race that was, at that point, ten minutes away.

Like Spartans bathing in oil, we prepared for the oncoming battle. As we did so, I noticed the source of my anxiety within the tent, its formation dispersed among the area, and walking over to ask if I wanted a picture. Unready to introduce my teammates to my family, I did what any rational person pressed for time before a race and full of pre-race energy would do, which was to quickly run over to the starting line to do the last strides of my cross country season before the race.

The air was still, its breeze slackened as if in anticipation for the impending shot and great mumbling of footsteps. The emotions, fear, anxiety, and hope all disappeared among the runners, whose eyes concentrated upon the referee. He carefully raised his gun, said "On your mark," and ...BANG! The race started.

The State Division Two Championship was in action, and I started the race like I wanted to start any race, with cautious optimism. Perhaps the same could be said of my attitude towards the future opinions of those exposed to my family structure. I like to think that people are capable of understanding and acceptance when they have the information to understand. Hopefully, the parents, children, and teammates who saw my polyamorous family thought of it with more than mere anxious tolerance.

Maybe they even regarded us with a sense of commonality—as families coming together to support their runners. Perhaps they did what our legal system, media, and religious authorities have not done: understanding someone who is different and caring for them anyway. Compassion is perhaps the most powerful tool one can have towards establishing community and thus I hoped that my teammates and society would understand.

I might have some explaining to do, but it would be dialogue that would serve a purpose.

But the race was underway, and the crowd of people gathered there to see it shouted names of various athletes, screaming such phrases as "Keep on going, you're doing awesome," or perhaps a bit less sporting: "COME ON YOU CAN CATCH HIM, YOU'RE A [insert mascot of school here], YOU CAN DO IT! RAWR!" The crowd was like a mass, chanting various phrases and praying to the clock that their child would beat their prior time.

For the athlete, it was just the race. Nothing more than sensation, a slew of grunting, taut sinews of pulsating muscles crashing together into the ground to fling a sweaty puppet forward. A Gaussian blur of footsteps on pavement thundering and shaking and droning with each unconscious step of each of the runners for each foot of the 3.1 miles. I was pushing, bedazzled by being in the moment, the race, the crucible of time and techniques of many days and hours, burning in a blaze of shouting, screaming, and dust. Pain was but a mere whisper within the thundering crash of my will, pushing my body to defy itself and defy my expectations. I was running away from time, but to the beat of a clock; at each moment both intensely aware of the importance of every single second, yet also hating each tick and breath and cycle of movements as they meant that I was not done and that my time was continuing to bleed. Approaching the halfway point was a temporary reprieve from the productive anxiety that controlled my body and inhabited my mind, providing a moment of scope, that the race was half over, that I was soon to be done. Yet the eye in the hurricane eventually stopped, pressing tiring limbs still further into submission, moving my legs to the command of instinct and the approval of self-motivation. The four-hundred-meter mark eventually brought forth the final rush of pain, agony, pride, and delight, and the suspension of all of the earth that was out of my path. It summoned a hibernating kick, moving my legs faster and faster, with no thought or strategy, charging, flailing, and moving so quickly that the pain of it all was suppressed by the thrill of the final stretch; the clock ticked and ticked and my feet leapt farther each second to defy the primordial opponent that I could not comprehend nor understand yet taunted me with each tick and screamed at my face that I could not do it, and I screamed and pushed and dashed and ran and ran and stopped.

I was done.

I looked around; my teammates were also finished, smiles of contentment and closure erupting from their faces. Sure we didn't do well, but it was over at last! Finally we could go back to our tent, quenched with a cocktail of air, sweat, and pain, with the knowledge that the season was over, and all the accompanying wistfulness and joy that it evoked in us. I too was engulfed by the feelings, and did not notice until five minutes afterward that my family arrived, that people didn't seem to react that adversely to my family after all; ironically, people seemed indifferent to it. However, that view was from my neurochemically drunk state of mind. What mattered was that I was done, and could finally look back upon how far I had come from when I had first started the sport. There I was, the senior in the top seven grasping at how far I had come. I had fear, but fear that was softened by the knowledge that it was not my concern that my family somehow wasn't "proper." My family was mine. And they loved and still love me. The number of people within my family was and is irrelevant; what matters is that there is care. And there was.

Eventually the wind returned, and with it came a sobering winter chill, the necessary precursor to an oncoming winter. The days shortened, and the darkness spread. But with it came the safe retreat to home, welcome and safe. The impending cold will come, but, like my season, that day and each day will pass. Time runs out.

Excerpts from an interview with Jack, age six

E. and Jack

JANUARY 27, 2015

Okay, Jack, all of the questions I'm going to ask you in this interview are about one topic: Our family. The first question I have is: What is a family?
Well, like a group of people that lives together.

That's a good answer. How would you describe our family? What are some words or phrases that you'd use to describe us?
Nice. And loud!

So true ... What's your favorite thing about being in our family? What's good about it?
Well, I like when you come home.

Aww, that's nice, thanks. I like coming home.
I like playing with your baby.

Yeah, I like it too. I'm glad you're such a good big brother.
I try.

What are some things we do as a family that you like to do?
Play fun games.

Like what?
Operation.

Anything else we do as a family that you like?
I like when we have pizza parties.

Oh, me too. That's one of my favorite things. You know what other thing I really like doing as a family (although we haven't done it in a little while)?
What is it?

Camping. Do you like camping as a family?
Yes, I like that. A lot.

What's one of the hardest things about being in our family?
That I have to clean up every day! It's true. And I'd rather be doing fun games and things.

Yeah…

(Then Jack hijacks the interview…)
Do you feel that way too? Do you feel this way: Would you rather be spending time with us and playing fun games instead of going to work? Is that the way you feel sometimes?

It is the way I feel sometimes. I think having to be away from you all day every day is probably one of the hardest parts of being in our family. But I like working, so it's okay.

Do you ever like tidying? Do you feel good when you finish?
Yes, because then I get to do fun stuff.

Yeah, but do you ever feel proud of yourself? Like, "Wow! That room looks so good because I spent a lot of time and energy making it look pretty." Do you ever feel that way?
Yes, and let me tell you a secret... (Whispers) Sometimes I like to get up when everyone else is asleep and tidy the house and then go back to bed.

Wow. So, it feels good to do something that helps out?
Yes.

That's really great. Okay, my next question is: what makes our family different from other families?
Hmm, I may have to think about that one for a minute.

Okay.
Well ... we keep our Christmas tree up a long time.

We do. Is there anything else you can think of? (Lots of thinking.) Who's another family that you know? What about the Thompson family? What makes them different from our family?
Well, they sell things at the Farmers Market, but we're not to that yet.

That's true. That's a good difference. Anything else? How many children do they have?
One.

How many children do we have?
Four.

How many parents do they have?
Two.

How many parents do we have?
Three.

So those are some differences, right?
Right.

Can you tell me something nice about each of the members
of our family?
*I'm usually really nice to my brothers and sister. M. makes
me laugh. W. is cute. V. is cute too. Mama makes good dinners.
Daddy is weird and funny. And you birthed a cute baby!*

Ha! I tried.

Thanks for letting me interview you, Jack. It was really
interesting to me.
You're welcome.

My parents' friends

Alexander Malcolm

My parents have some friends that are my friends too! My mommy's friend's name is Lee. Usually at nights they go out to a restaurant and eat some food. When Lee is at my house, we play on my OUYA (a game console) together. I know my mom has other friends but I'm just talking about Lee.

My dad's friend's name is Jasmine. She is from the Philippines. I don't know why they are friends but who cares? I don't see Jasmine very often but she sends me some postcards. I keep forgetting to e-mail her probably because there are lots of fun things to do.

Now that I live in the U.S. I won't see them as often. But my parents might get new friends.

Our normal family

Angela Callais

This is the story of how our big queer weird family is actually, more often than not, pretty normal too. Sometimes it's hard to define where my family begins and where it ends, and it's certainly tricky to describe it!

My family is queer in orientation, in gender and in configuration. In other ways, we're just plain regular. We eat dinners together, we do homework, we like doing puzzles together (well, some of us more than others). My daughter Quinn is thirteen years old and a very awesome kid. My wife Denise and I have been together for six years. We were monogamous for the first eighteen months of our relationship, and then moved into an open, polyamorous relationship for the last four and a half years.

When the concept of polyamory was first introduced to me over a decade ago, I had a knee-jerk reaction that it wasn't for me, that I would be Too Jealous (whatever that means!). But I'm a curious person, so I decided to learn more and I set out on my own personal research project. I read books, listened to podcasts, found articles and blogs on the Internet. Everything that I read and listened to actually made a lot of sense, but I still wasn't sure that it was right for me. At that point in time, I decided it wasn't and I was okay with that decision.

Years later, I am as surprised as anyone to say that I identify as polyamorous!

Our family stumbled into this. It started out as what we sometimes refer to as "fun sexy adventures," which basically meant that we had opened our relationship up to include the possibility of having sex with other people, both together as a couple and individually. We laid some ground rules around honesty (we wanted to know the details of the adventure) and safety (safer sex practices only). We were clear to also say that one of the most important rules was NO FALLING IN LOVE. After all, this was just fun sexy adventures. Right? Right!

This worked well for both of us for a while...and then I fell in love with someone else. *This was not in the plan!* When I was with this great new person, Wallace, I felt this giddy, amazing, fun and deepening connection with her. I was having a great time getting to know her—we were talking for hours, having sex for hours. I was very much enjoying her company.

And when I was with Denise, I felt the same way that I had felt about her from the beginning—a shocking amount of "WOW!" She is one of the most incredible people that I have ever met; kind, generous, great to look at, talented in many ways, someone that I trust implicitly and love more than I could ever have imagined. Nothing had changed.

And yet, I had broken the rules. I felt so scared to tell Denise, because I didn't know if she would believe me when I said that I had fallen in love with this other person and somehow...I still loved her the same. Was this possible? It felt like the truth, but every message that I had received throughout my life was that you only romantically love one person at a time. I had been told that if you started to love someone else, then that was the evidence that confirmed that something was wrong with your current relationship. I felt so confused. I was so scared of hurting or losing Denise.

But I had to tell her.

Thankfully (precisely because she is so amazing)—she already knew. She had been getting to know Wallace too, right alongside me. The three of us had spent time together, and the two of them had even gone fishing on their own.

Denise knows me. She had been listening to me. She had the grace and kindness to tell me that she could see what had been happening, and that while it was new and weird it was okay with her. She knew I still loved her. And she still loved me too. It was exactly what I needed to hear.

Once that conversation had taken place, it changed a lot of things about our lives. There were some friends who knew about our "adventures" and there were some who didn't. It made it complicated to know what to share and with whom. We don't share information about our sex lives with our family, co-workers and even most friends. However, we do share information about our significant relationships with those people, and that's where it got tricky.

Up until this point, my time with Wallace had been a secret from many people in my life. But Wallace wasn't somebody to hide, she was important to me as my girlfriend. We had crossed over into a place where it felt wrong to hide our relationship, yet scary to tell people—primarily out of the fear of judgment.

We started by having a conversation with our daughter, who was then nine years old. Beforehand, Denise and I talked through all of the possible scenarios and reactions that we could think of. We felt as prepared as we could be, but we also felt completely terrified! How in the world was she going to take this?!

Later that week, we were all lying on our bed together snuggling with our cat when we told Quinn that we needed to talk with her about something important. I started by pointing out that we knew many different kinds of families: different gender configurations, religions, married, divorced, single, etc. We talked about our family values of people being free to do what felt good to them as long as there was consent and how that looked different for everyone. At this point she was getting somewhat antsy and bored, because this was a message she had heard a million times before.

Then I said, "Do you remember Wallace?" Quinn had previously met Wallace at the beach with a group of our friends. She said that she did. I told her that Wallace was not just my friend, but my girlfriend. "Oh," she said. I told her that Denise and I had talked about it and that we had decided to open our relationship up to other people. I said that we both felt very good about it, and we wanted to include her and make sure that she knew what was happening and hear her thoughts about it as well. I explained that Denise and I were still married, that our family would still live in the same house and that we didn't plan for anything to change in our life at home. But that Wallace was my girlfriend.

There was a very long pause.

"You guys are so weird!" she exclaimed, complete with eye roll.

"Do you have any questions about it all?" I asked.

"Not really. Can I go watch my show now?"

"Sure."

We couldn't believe it. In hindsight, I'm not totally sure what we were expecting, but it definitely wasn't that. I sat on it, assuming that she needed more time to process and that surely a negative reaction would come at some point.

Guess what? It's been four years and I'm still waiting for it.

So where are we now? My relationship with Wallace ran its course. I still care about her and see her as a friend from time to time. I have been with my boyfriend, Nolan, for the last two years. He is a very significant person in my life, and subsequently my family's lives. Our deepening relationship has contributed to our family coming out even more widely to include the dynamics of extended family members and family holiday events, as well as questioning and changing the hierarchical ways that we had started out structuring our relationship (using terms such as primary, secondary, etc.). Denise has been with her girlfriend (who prefers to remain unnamed), for the last two years. We also occasionally date others. Our relationships are all continually evolving in a way that is challenging, exciting and fulfilling, all at the same time.

While Denise and I have dated many people with varying degrees of seriousness over the last four years, our relationship, Quinn's life and our home have remained very stable. Over the years, Quinn has met some of the people we have dated, and others she hasn't. We are social people, so having friends and family over isn't a strange occurrence at our house. Quinn herself is a complete extrovert, so she is always up for another person who would like to listen to her!

In preparation for this story, I decided it would be a great idea for Denise and I to interview Quinn. She is now a vibrant, tenacious, opinionated and chatty thirteen-year-old. Certainly she would give me great fodder about all of the ways that being in a polyamorous family has changed her life!

It was—again—surprisingly anticlimactic.

That conversation that we agonized over beforehand, the one where we told her we were opening up our relationship? She doesn't remember it. Well, she remembers that we told her, but she doesn't remember any of the details and we all had a good laugh together when we explained it again.

We tried asking her multiple questions, rewording questions, trying to hook something of significance. She kept answering that it just doesn't end up being a big deal to her. She believes that people can do what they want, and that it's not up to her to decide what is right for others, especially if it isn't directly affecting her negatively. She doesn't believe that being in a polyamorous family affects her negatively in any way.

When I asked her if it affected her positively, she started laughing and said, "This may sound kinda selfish, but it's more people to give me presents and buy me things! That's an upside!"

I asked her what happens when it comes up around her friends, such as when Nolan is around our family and someone says, "Hey, who is Nolan?"

"I say, my mom's boyfriend," she replies. "And then they're like, wait—what? They always get really confused," she says, laughing. "They're like, did something happen that you didn't tell me? And I'm like no, it's just another person, and they're like, oh . . . .okay. Most of the time people are so dumbfounded. I'll say—no, it's her boyfriend and they just get caught up on the fact that I tell them that no, nothing happened and they're still like ....your mom and Denise are divorced." She keeps laughing and continues on, "I just say—nope, they have an open relationship!"

Lastly, I asked her how she thought people should talk to their kids about it.

She replied, "I think that's kind of hard, because it depends on the kid. I feel like it depends on the situation that the family is in, and the views that the child has. If they are more like me who doesn't really care at all, and doesn't really have an opinion, I would say try to tell them as honestly as possible. Just be like, yeah, this is what's happening. How do you feel about it? Let them know that you are going to take what they think into account, but it's not going to change your overall decision.

"If they know their kids have been iffy about the whole thing, and their kid is feeling weird about that and not really sure, I would try to ease into it more instead of just having a conversation and telling them what's happening. Especially if it happens really quickly, you would want to be more careful about how you are approaching that topic. I would tell my kids, it may be confusing that you have a dad now and now I have a girlfriend too, especially if they are young and didn't know what bi meant or lesbian or heterosexual then I would try to explain it to them as best I could and be like I'm bisexual which means I like men and women and we have decided that we want to be a polyamorous family or an open family which means that we are open to having more people come into our love lives that doesn't mean we love each other any less we still love you the same our love is going equally to everybody we are just not cheating on anyone. I think the biggest thing for anybody is the feeling of cheating. I feel like maybe that is me, but I feel like that is the biggest deal, especially if you start out as just two people and then spread out. Focus on that this does not mean that I love anyone else any less, this just means that we are open to loving more people and adding more people to this family and we hope that it is okay with you too."

(Does your teenager talk in massive run-on sentences too? When does she breathe?!)

One of the greatest things about polyamory is also one of the hardest things about polyamory: there is no well-worn path that is easy to find or follow in this lifestyle. The pop-culture narrative rarely holds true for day-to-day life, and those of us living polyamorously each do it in our own way, with our own variations. While there is a certain amount of freedom and relief in this, there is also a lot of confusion about the "right" way to do things, and it's particularly hard when you don't know how to start or where to go next. Find community, online or in person. Communicate openly and honestly. Be who you are. If you stay true to yourself you will find your way, and you might just find that you are actually one big queer weird family that is actually shockingly normal too.

Part IV: Things fall apart

KIMCHI CUDDLES.com

#333 "Transitions and Support"

Mom, my partner and I are transitioning our relationship and he's thinking about moving out

WHAT? You're breaking up??

Well, we're TRANSITIONING to something different. We're not sure yet what it will look like, but we're trying to do it as LOVINGLY as possible...

You have KIDS together! How could he do this to you??

He's not doing something TO me. We're both doing our best to find something that works for both of us right now

I've got your back, sweety! He'll NEVER be allowed near our house!

That's not helping! The transition is hard, but it doesn't need to be ANGRY. we're trying to do this lovingly, together

The only way I know how to support you is by HATING him

Moments

Dominica Malcolm

Living in Malaysia in a polyamorous marriage is a lot harder as a woman than it is for a man, at least in my experience. My husband has had a Filipino girlfriend for years and the only men I've met who are interested in me are would-be cheaters. The single men I meet are scared of the idea of my husband knowing about us—cheating and monogamy seem to be the only acceptable options. I'm resigned to only making friends, and with my interests, they tend to be men.

I start spending one-on-one time with Lee after realising that he's tried to include me in conversations for months when others haven't made the same effort. I also recall him telling me, for the second time, that he enjoyed seeing me on stage years ago. Lee discusses movies a lot, and my previously movie-rich life has been sorely lacking since having children. I think it would be nice to have a new movie buddy—and his schedule means that I can watch movies with him while my husband works.

*

It's February; three months into my friendship with Lee, and my husband quit his job with nothing lined up. Lee knows that much, and my husband and I figured we would still be able to stay in Malaysia until our visas expired, giving us plenty of time to find something else, possibly having to move somewhere else. We were wrong.

I send a panicked message to Lee. *FUCK FUCK FUCK. Jeremy just told me some really fucked up shit. We may have to leave the country before October.*

Ten minutes later, Lee responds. *What?! That's it? So quick ... Wow. I really don't know what to say right now. Once I'm done with the show, we'll meet okay? That'll be on Sunday. Relax and don't let this take you down okay? Talk to me.*

I explain a little of what's going on, and add, *We might try and stay using Malaysia My Second Home, but if we decide to do that, I'd really like some help finding a place for us to move to. Do you think you might be able to help me with that?*

Lee replies, *Of course! Anything to help you guys get through this. Heck, if you say the words I'm sure the whole community would also lend a hand. Don't hold back! Your mind must be mushed right now, but take things one at a time okay? You can get through this.*

*

It's Sunday, and I'm holding back the emotion from escaping my eyes, avoiding the prospect of leaving as best as I can. Lee is sitting opposite me at my dining table while my husband is out with our kids and his girlfriend. I need the privacy to vent about everything that's been happening, but then our conversation switches to one of our favourite topics.

"I loved *She's All That* because I could relate to Rachael Leigh Cook's character. The shy, dorky girl. I never got the transformation she got, though," I say.

"Yeah, but she was better before the transformation. Same with Anne Hathaway in *The Princess Diaries*."

I laugh. "Yeah, agreed. I can't believe you've seen those films."

"I watch everything, remember? Besides, that's the kind of girl I'm attracted to." Lee's face scrunches up in a smile, and I can't help but wonder for probably the hundredth time if he's still attracted to me.

I recall a conversation from a month ago, about when he first saw me on stage. He told me then, "I wanted to come talk to you after the show, but I was too shy."

Because he had remembered me for years, and enjoyed one of my worst performances to date, I asked, "Were you attracted to me?"

Lee confessed, then, "Yeah, I was."

"Have you seen *A Goofy Movie*?" I ask, and Lee nods. "I watched that movie so many times when I was in high school. I felt so much like Max," I say, referring to Goofy's son, who was yet another dorky high school character.

"I loved the soundtrack," Lee admits.

"No way! I was about to say exactly that. I wish I owned it. I love the soundtrack so much. The music really captured how I felt in high school."

"Powerline's songs especially."

I nod enthusiastically, and feel a rush of energy enter my body from the inside out. Never before have I met anyone who loves *A Goofy Movie* as much as I do. Oh, God. I think I'm definitely crushing now. I can't tell Lee that, though, can I?

*

We get together a few times over the next three weeks, and my mind is a battleground for how much I should say. Winding myself up and stepping back. Flirting with Lee, pushing boundaries as I've done throughout the friendship. I always enjoy teasing him for his inexperience, just to see his face flip out and have him pretend he's going to run away because I've made things awkward. But now I'm in bed most of the weekend, having gotten sick after chatting to Lee for seven hours until after two in the morning in my air-conditioned apartment while my husband was overseas for work. My husband has accepted a job in San Francisco, and we know now that my family and I will be moving. I decide it's time to finally try and say something, so I send Lee a message.

I'm starting to feel like this illness is punishment for me holding back the other night rather than saying what's on my mind. Can I tell you what that was about and hope it doesn't make things (bad) awkward between us? I'm leaving soon anyway so maybe it doesn't matter if it does have that effect.

Lee replies, *Sure, since I'm relatively safe here at home. Shoot!*

Yeah, that's what I'm thinking, safety of my own home, and I can avoid going to the next few shows if I make things bad, I write. *Though I do hope that doesn't happen.*

I'm so nervous that I just sit at my computer for several minutes before I figure out the exact phrasing to compose.

So. Basically, in the beginning, me pushing the line was just for fun, because I liked seeing you squirm. It made me laugh. But I think as time has gone on that line has gotten blurred and I didn't know if I was having a laugh or being serious. Clearly now, though, I'm holding myself back because I'm scared. Scared of wanting more from you than what we have now. Scared of you not wanting to talk to me anymore.

When Lee doesn't respond for an hour, I fear the worst. Then I see the notification, and I'm almost too scared to read his reply.

Woah, well, I kinda had a small feeling that you might feel this way but suppressed it immediately. But now since you've said it (brave move I have to admit, and see, you ARE the adult in this friendship) I don't know what to do really. I kinda liked how things have been moving naturally for us. It's just that I never thought it would come to this. It feels kinda nice, scary and bewildering all at the same time. I guess I'm on the fence on this relationship as well.

I'm in a natural mix of joy and surprise. This is the last thing I expected Lee to say. I'm impressed by how well he read between the lines.

Lee adds, *Also, don't worry about me running off and not talking to you.*

I smile a lot as I type my reply. *That's, um, not the reaction I was expecting, given my anxiety and all that. Though funnily enough, the illness I've been feeling the last few days seems to be about gone now, so there you go. So. Um. I wasn't imagining things? That's good to know. It's hard to tell with all those mixed signals we keep giving each other :P I'm not saying we need to act on this. Honestly, the fact I'm moving giving me a time limit on this is basically what I hate most about the fact I can't stay. I was happy to just let things develop naturally if that's what was going to happen. I guess in the end I just decided it was better for you to know rather than keep it in and not give it a chance.*

I picture Lee as I read his response, *You see, in my mind keeping it all bottled in is the way to go. Maybe it's that Asian-y method of saving face first, your feelings second. But it's nice to play around those boundaries for once in my life. Feels like being an adult for a change. Shy boy and girl, awkwardness, time limit. Sounds like a really bad rom com doesn't it?*

*

It's four weeks later, and we've gotten over the hurdle of actually physically touching each other, and making out…there's been plenty of that by now. We're presented with the probability of not seeing each other for an entire week, since I have a resort booked in Cherating, a beach that is roughly a three-and-a-half to four-hour drive away from where I live in Kuala Lumpur. Meanwhile, Lee has various work engagements during both the start and end of that week, so he can't even keep me and the kids company while my husband is overseas for a conference.

It's a day into the vacation, and I'm already sending desperate messages to Lee.

I think I might tear my hair out and go insane if I have to spend all week here with the kids on my own. That or maybe check out early.

Woah…must be one hella trip. How ya holding up so far? Lee asks.

I'm about ready to jump off the balcony, honestly. I can be that direct with Lee. He knows about my battle with depression. This is the worst I've felt since going on medication for it. *There's nothing for the kids to do in the room but they won't let me drive them somewhere more interesting. Or even to go buy food so I don't have to keep feeding them at the hotel restaurant. This morning was okay with them playing at the playground and me reading on my Kindle. But I don't think I can do that for the whole week.*

Isolation is the worst.

Lee replies, *Yikes! That's not good at all… As long as the kids are occupied and not bored out of their mind that's okay. But you on the other hand…who's taking care of you?*

I can't help but hope that's a sign he'll drive out to see us the first chance he gets, in between his prior commitments, but I'm used to disappointment from friends not coming to things I invite them to, so I can't hope too much.

Messages in this vein continue for the next day and a half. Lee's finished with his commitments for a couple of days, so I'm desperate to get him to visit. He tells me he's not in a good mood, but maybe tomorrow, he can come for one night only.

I text him, *If I called you and you could hear my voice, would that do a better job of convincing you to come today?*

Lee replies instantly, *I'm gonna go out soon and do some chores, so I'll call you once I'm done okay? Hang tight. And I'm sorry for all this. I really am.*

Patience is not my strong suit, but since my phone is running out of battery life, I plug it in to charge and let my youngest play games on it. It's the easiest way to avoid trying to contact him. I grab my Kindle and sit in bed, reading. I get so wrapped up in the book that I don't notice the hours ticking by.

It's five thirty when I finally check the time. I'd have expected Lee to call me by now. Could he be on his way here? I try not to think about that, so I gather the kids together and take them up to the restaurant for an early dinner.

As soon as we're done ordering, Lee finally calls.

"Where are you at the moment?" he asks.

"In the restaurant," I say. "Why? You're not here, are you?" My heart starts pounding out of my chest at the thought. "Oh my God, are you here?"

"No," he says, and my heart sinks into my stomach.

We continue talking while the kids and I wait for dinner to arrive.

Then the unthinkable happens. Lee is standing right next to our table, carrying an overnight bag. He's dressed for the beach, and I feel like I'm smiling from ear to ear.

"Look who's here, kids," I say with an enormous smile.

Both my sons jump up and down in their chairs and shout Lee's name. After all the time he's spent playing video games with them in the past few months, they're just as excited to see him as I am.

*

I sit at the picnic table watching Lee push the boys on the swings at the playground, just admiring how he does it all with a genuine smile on his face. We go back to our room and fetch the kids' beach toys, then head to the beach for the first time since we arrived. I sit in the dry, white sand and watch as Lee takes the boys closer to the sea and helps them build sandcastles with the wet sand. I don't want this to end. I don't want to leave him behind when I move to America. I didn't plan any of this, but here I am, falling in love with Lee.

*

My husband is already in San Francisco, organising things for our new home. I'm in bed with Lee, taking in his face, and the way the sides of his eyes wrinkle when he smiles at me. It's time to have a complicated conversation that I haven't known how to bring up. But it needs to happen, because we haven't been using protection.

"I don't think it's cause to worry yet, but my period is due, and I haven't got it yet. I'm usually right on schedule. What will we do if you accidentally get me pregnant?" I ask.

He takes a couple of seconds, then says with sincerity, "Well, I wouldn't make you get an abortion."

That's nice to know, but it doesn't really cover the most important point. The one I've been mulling over in my mind for a while.

I snuggle my head against Lee's chin and shoulder, and wrap an arm around his chest. "Okay, but, I mean...even if I don't say anything, people are going to know it's not Jeremy's. It'll be half Chinese—at the very least, there's no way it'll have blue eyes like me and him. I know you don't want people to know about us, but I'd have to tell people at some point."

"Well I guess my mom would be happy to finally have grandchildren."

"What? You'd tell her about us? I thought your family wouldn't accept our relationship?"

"I'll just have to explain it to her. Over a month."

We begin hashing out the complexities of the possibility of me giving birth to his child in another country, however slim the chance. The more he seems open to telling people about us, the more I start thinking about how much I could see a long future between us. I realise that's exactly what I want. I want him to join our family in San Francisco.

*

Lee and I have another great month together before I fly to San Francisco with the kids, but we're not together now. He lost his trust in me a month after the move, when he learned I told a mutual friend about us. It's been months since I tried to talk to him, and another month and a half since he stopped talking to me.

I can't help going back over that moment our relationship changed forever. When I wrote to him, *I'm scared. Scared of you not wanting to talk to me anymore.* And he wrote back, *Don't worry about me running off and not talking to you.*

My deepest fear about our relationship has become a reality, and I've lost one of the best friends I've ever had.

It's the moments of great friendship and connection I miss most. How much he helped me with the kids. Playing video games, and building sandcastles. Coming to the eldest one's birthday party at the last minute because no one else would have otherwise. Discovering both our love for *A Goofy Movie*, and its soundtrack. All the movies we enjoyed and referenced together.

The fantasy of who Lee became to me wasn't real. Although things didn't work out between us, he really showed me what I need in a polyamorous family. If I am to find another partner, I want it to be someone who can have that same connection with my children. Someone who shares interests with me that my husband does not. But, most importantly, no longer will I settle for secrecy. I deserve to be known to my partner's friends and family the way I am with my husband's.

Once upon a time on my birthday, or being poly does not mean I have no boundaries

Aoife Lee

That's how it all started. Once upon a time on my birthday, my husband brought your girlfriend home as my present. Complicated, right? Welcome to the polycule.

I remember hearing about you that weekend—sitting at the kitchen table listening to her talk about this wonderful man with whom she was so happy. Sending home with her at the end of the weekend bread I had baked for us all. Hearing later in the week how much you liked it. Trading funny comments with one another on her FB in the coming months.

It wasn't until months later that I actually met you. I remember that moment so well, so somatically. I remember the anticipation all the way from the airport when she picked us up for that long weekend. I remember the butterflies in my stomach, the tension in my shoulders. I remember knowing that this was someone who I wanted to like me. Someone I had come to recognize as smart, a fellow history buff, a nerd, witty, and with a love of language to beat even mine. And we walked into the house, through the basement, and in a doorway we almost bumped into one another. Months later you would tell me that I seemed standoffish in that moment. It was not my intent, I was just so nervous!

I fell in like with you online, in lust with you that weekend, and was well and truly on the way to love by the time we flew home at the end of it. It's true. Those hours spent talking, sharing stories of our lives, families, beloved books, academic memories, likes, and dislikes . . . they were just as good as the long hours spent learning one another's bodies. That we all had that weekend together—the four of us eating that wonderful meal, watching favorite movies, cuddled on the floor because the sofa just wasn't big enough. I can still picture you and my husband sitting at the kitchen counter while your girlfriend and I made dinner. You were eating popcorn—was the show really that entertaining? I have no idea what was so funny, but remember clearly being hysterical with laughter, and at one point threatening to pour the popcorn over someone's head???

I know, it sounds idyllic. It wasn't. This was unexpected. I expected to like you, to spend the weekend having fun and hopefully some flirting and sex with two good friends. I never expected to fall in love. I can admit it, I developed tunnel vision—I forgot to pay attention to how my husband might be impacted at times. I remember him coming to me and needing to cry and process after seeing me lying in your arms and talking for long periods. This had not been something I had shared with someone other than him before. In my infatuation it hadn't even occurred to me to think about this.

So we fell in love. I could tell the whole story, but it happened fast. Within weeks we were a daily part of each other's lives, albeit at a distance. Two months later you came to visit for a week—a blissful week of relaxation, companionship, time off work, and time (for me) with the two people with whom I was madly in love!

You went home to chaos and heartbreak. Your relationship ended in a way that hurt you terribly. I helped you in every way that I could. I really do not believe I am flattering myself in saying that I helped put you back together. Seeing you look back and identify things that hurt you, that you wanted to be different in new relationships, seeing you make a new home for yourself, a new career, a new life ... it was a joy to support you in that. I was so excited to see you succeed and move towards being loved and valued for the wonderful individual you are.

So we survived that. We remained in a relationship—I was your girlfriend, you were my boyfriend. I was married, you were "single," but in a committed relationship with me. You were, from the beginning, incredibly respectful of my relationship with B, considering him a friend and recognizing that you would never want to threaten that relationship (nor would I let you). We survived my getting laid off and making a big career change. We survived your new job stresses, dealing with insomnia, dealing with being far apart, days that we were not able to talk or write... We visited. We found our own ways to spend time together. I will never forget watching TV "together" by pressing play on Netflix at the same moment, or hearing you read your favorite books to me before bed at night. Long distance was torture, but these things helped. I thought we were doing it just right.

I thought we were doing it right when you asked me if I was okay with you reading to a new friend with whom you were communicating. It hurt my heart a little bit, but I was so proud that we were practicing what we preached— open communication, talking about things before there was a problem, we were getting it right!

I thought we were getting it right when you started dating M, and she was initially so respectful of your relationship with me. When she and I got into long, funny, excitable, and silly conversations on FB (which you occasionally witnessed in terror as we planned public outings for the three of us—you being hauled along in the wake of two silly, overexcited, costume-obsessed nerd girls!). Yes, I was scared. I was so in love with you, and so happy with what we had. I was afraid that you would get all your needs met by her, that you wouldn't need me anymore. I was afraid of losing you, but I was also hopeful that we could all grow in love/friendship/support/companionship together.

Sadly, it was not to be. Long story short, as your relationship with her grew, my relationship with you seemed to become more and more threatening to her. Dividing your time was not easy, but you managed it. We each shared with you when we were frustrated with that, sometimes productively, other times manipulatively. I know it was hard for you when both of us were upset—I had experienced that, trying to work out which partner to care for when both were in need.

She wrote to me over and over and over that she would "never" ask you to give me up, but then her behavior asked or demanded that time and again. Over time my interactions with her conveyed to me that I was disliked, mistrusted, and unwanted—that she would be happier were I to disappear from your life, and was unwilling to work towards sharing and compromise. I do not want to imply that the fault is all on any one party. I am aware of my own tendency to over-interpret anger or slights. And I am afraid that there are things you wanted that you felt you could not ask me for. I am scared that having talked about some of those might have prevented some of the hurt and the distance I felt growing between us. I am horrified, and almost ashamed to call myself a therapist, when I look at the appalling failure of communication that the three of us managed to create.

The more protective she became of your relationship, the less you and I talked about it. I remained unaware that this was such a wonderful development (which I really would have liked to know), and we were not able to talk about how it was gradually impacting the way you and I interacted in small ways. Each insignificant in the moment, but adding up. And eventually I realized that there was something that was the most important thing in your life that you didn't share with me at all. I began to be able to tell when you were thinking about it, when it was stressing you out ... Hell, the reason (I think) that you told me about your decision to change our relationship when you did was because *I asked you* what was bothering you. I had known in my heart for twenty-four hours that you were working up to breaking up with me.

After eighteen months of love, friendship, and companionship, you told me that you needed to change the status of our relationship. You explained that this was about labels and sex, but "nothing to do with how I feel about you." That you wanted to keep all the emotional intimacy we shared, but no longer be romantic partners. At the end of a wonderful week together, you shared this the night before I was to leave. You told me that in order to move forward with your relationship with M, you needed for our relationship to change in this way. You broke up with me, but wanted to remain the best friend you had become, though we were never "just friends."

Though I could not see it until months later, the hardest part of this was not losing our relationship. The hardest part was the assumption you had that it would somehow be easy for me to contort myself into a different shape to suit the needs of your new relationship. That it would not hurt me to give up all our romantic traditions or activities. And in the aftermath of the initial shock, the realization of how that new relationship had already eroded what we had. I think this realization surprised us both. I don't think you were expecting me to come to you with those observations and demand to know what evidence there was that our relationship (which you insisted we could still have, just not sexually) would not continue to waste away under those pressures.

For three months we tried to reconnect and negotiate new boundaries that would allow us to remain intimate friends. Eventually I could only come to the conclusion that I was not interested in a relationship with someone in whose life I could only exist when their partner was not present. To me the idea of "confidant" meant a person I could call when the shit hits the fan—the way I called you the day I got laid off. If I had to check a calendar to see whether I can make that phone call or not . . . that's not it. Constantly having to try to reconnect and then hitting an embargo period left me feeling tossed aside for something shinier and then having to start all over.

We limped on as long as we could, out of the knowledge on both of our parts that our lives were just not right without one another. But neither was my life right with an inauthentic version of you. Nor could I live without authenticity … nor was I willing to sacrifice it, that thing you once told me you fell in love with in me.

B had a role in the end of our relationship also. He was, is, and will remain my rock. The level of understanding, compassion, and patience he displayed as I mourned this incredible loss is beyond words. He held me as I cried, reassured me as I contemplated possible courses of action, and supported my decision without trying to influence it. While poly was the sticking point in my relationship with you, the presence of my primary relationship made it possible for me to stand up for myself. Having the love and support of my partner, as well as the feedback of patterns he saw in our interactions, provided more than I could have asked for from anyone.

The honest truth about how I felt about you was anathema to the person you loved. The honest truth about what I wanted from you was more than you were willing or able to give.

Even as I wrote those words to you I kept hoping that if I could just say the right thing, do something different, that somehow we could find a way to be authentically in each other's lives again. I wanted to be embraced by your life again, but no matter how badly I wished for that, it was not in me to wish for the end of your new, primary, relationship.

I wrote to you that "I would rather cry every day of my life than lose you. But that is not a way to live my life. Nor can I prevent that loss—it has happened already." You wrote back that there was a place in your soul that was forever mine, a place that lit up when I was there, and that would never be shut to me.

It has been almost two years now, and I hope that is still true. I know there remains a corner of my heart with a you-shaped hole in it. That place in my heart will always be exclusively yours, though I will always have room for others as well. I will always think of you when I eat bacon, when I watch *Star Wars*, when I make history jokes, and when I catch a glimpse of red in my hair. I will see shadows of you in my home, feel your arms around me on cold nights, and want to hear your voice and opinions on most topics that I come across. I will always want to see you, always want to share with you, and always want to be loved by you. Because being loved by you was an amazing, beautiful experience in my life.

Do I regret my decision? Do I regret having to set a boundary? Actually, no. It was horrible and hard, and I do still miss you daily (more on harder days—I miss my best friend). But hearing through the grapevine of your continuing happiness, I think I made the right decision for myself. I suspect that M is more comfortable, though that was never my motivation. But I wish you joy in your monogamy, and I hope it is really what *you* want. And I hope that you have a measure of peace, and can look back on me as someone who loved you well, and always will.

Our story is about love—that will always be the biggest feature of our tale for me. It is about strength and truth too, and making hard choices. And it is about poly and non-poly. Not in a competitive sense, but perhaps our story is about how poly ended one relationship for me. But perhaps it is about how without poly I would never have had that relationship in the first place, nor have had the strength to set a boundary in a relationship that was hurting me.

Losing my boyfriend's girlfriend

Louisa Leontiades

It's a fact. Polyamory provides mind-altering perspective. That's not to say it's the only challenge in this world which does, nor that it's 'better' than any other relationship paradigm. But it challenges you in ways you could never imagine. One of them is when your boyfriend goes out and falls in love with someone stunningly beautiful.

Because in this world there *are* stunning women. Long luscious locks, superb pocket Venus bodies, smooth yet chiselled beauties. Like a *Cosmo* cover or a J. Lo but unairbrushed. In the flesh. These women live surrounded by money. They love and laugh in glitter. They go to the gym and take care of their bodies. They have attitude and dance like tigers. They experience the world through travel, movement and socialization.

The thing is that I was once one of those women. Oh, I was never chiselled like her. I definitely needed the airbrushing. But I was what they call 'in good nick'. I went to the gym. I travelled the world. It was an incredible period of my life. But I no longer inhabit that reality. I'm not an executive and I have long since left the party circuit. I live on an island with no shops, no cars and very little need for makeup. In the wild with my children, I'm a retired version of my former self, with cellulite and a flabby tummy.

I don't know the real J. Lo, of course, but there was a tiny part of me that imagined until recently I might be able to find something to dislike about her. That part comforted me in the loss of my old life and shapely body. That my Versace jacket languishes—unworn—in the storage box under my bed. Surely it's not possible to have a great personality as well as drop dead gorgeous looks? Surely she's bought into 'evil' consumerism that I abandoned? Surely I can justify my disdain on something more than my own pitiful envy? That tiny part of me existed peacefully, sparking and fizzing occasionally at the sight of the glossy magazines in the stands that I never buy anymore.

But then four months ago I met a J. Lo woman. She's a ten. Oh, is she a ten. I've seen her in her pyjamas and no makeup. She's still a ten. She's my boyfriend's new love.

At nearly forty, I love my life. But I look at my greying hair and my stretch-marked belly with pragmatism. I can be beautiful ... when I make the effort. Mostly it's a different definition of beauty. I am aging ... sometimes awkwardly and sometimes elegantly. I have only just abandoned G-strings five years after I should have called it a day. With age I become more comfortable about stating my preferences and living in my skin. I buy larger jeans without sighing (much). I attack life differently now. I used to tear out large chunks and gobble it up. But now my own private soundtrack to life is chilled. I'm more often in my own sanctuary than amid the chaos and glamour of life over on the child-free side.

It's a different kind of beauty from the one society teaches us.

I never expected to feel inadequate at this stage, nor to have life shove my inadequacy so brutally in my face in a period when I am confronted savagely by my own mortality through illness. In my fear and grief, I am brought still more conflict.

No, I wasn't prepared for this gift. Are we ever?

But she came my way in a package of abundant beauty and a whirlwind of emotion. A new mirror, eight years younger than me. Along with the awestruck admiration I felt at her dazzling appearance (and indeed my boyfriend's ability to attract such a creature) I felt pangs of envy. My waist was once that size. I once had the time to spend on myself, before the children. I once had the passion with my partner that she has now. At first I contemplated working out. Buying a new wardrobe. Dyeing my hair. But it's a contest I didn't want and would never win.

'You have an aura', she said to me once. 'I see you like an angel. The love coming off you makes a halo.'

She's beautiful in body and in soul. My real-life J. Lo wears her heart on her sleeve. She, like me, tastes life to every last morsel. She lives her passions as enormously as she can inside the restrictions that life has given her. She's a party animal. She dances like she lives. With abandon. When it's dark for her, it's very dark. It's at its darkest when she feels trapped. Like me. I know her. And because I know her, I love her.

We both crave freedom. We both feed off life like vampires. We both understand pain. And we understand what it is like to love the same man. That's a rare experience.

She has brought me gifts. The gift of envy. The gift of humility. The gift of acceptance. The gift of gratitude. The gift of love.

It's been said that to be ready for an open relationship you need already to be secure. But until you are faced with life's challenges there are few ways of knowing whether that is really the case. Let's suppose you aren't. Let's suppose that a post-birth tummy, cellulite and grey hair don't make you feel particularly attractive. Let's say that the hot white passion of attraction between you and your partner has mellowed into domestic bliss and squabbles.

Will you feel inadequate when faced with what you lost? Or will you embrace what you have?

Life is about growth. About facing and overcoming your demons. And so you have a choice. You can either appreciate what you are now and what you have now, realising that it is beautiful, or you can cling forever after to what you used to have, to who you used to be, competing with shadows of your past and never winning.

THE END

I sit with him. His head is bowed and he looks tired and sad. If tears could leak out of his eyes they would. But my boyfriend has been trained not to cry, although what he does when he's alone listening to his favourite love songs, even I'm not privy to. It's heartbreaking when someone who is so optimistic, so full of boundless positivity and who brings such joy to lives through his music, is in a pit of numbed nothingness. But it's not my heartbreak I'm concerned with, it's his.

In an open relationship you have experiences which are a rarity in other people's lives. You welcome jealousy as a teacher. You challenge what a relationship really means. But the questions that are asked and answered in the polyamorous literature rarely cover the topic . . . what to do when your boyfriend is grieving the loss of his lover.

I'm projecting of course as I always do. He's a 'coper'...
one of the reasons I love him. When we met he said about
my baggage...

'Don't worry darling, I can handle heavy.'

He's always been the dependable one.

Perhaps he doesn't feel what I feel, to the extent that
I think he's feeling it. I think he's feeling what I would be
feeling. But oh.

If it were me who'd broken up with him, I'd have some
anger, some justifiable explanation of why he was wrong
and I was right. But it's not me. I have no anger, no justifi-
cation. Nothing to water down the sorrow I feel. I try and
counter with some useless platitudes like, 'Well you'll find
someone else.' Or 'Why don't you go out on the town with
your mates?' But in the end, I just keep quiet and listen.

'She changed. Here one minute, the girl who was
brimming with love and then her heart switched off. This
girl, I don't know her. So it's not her now I'm grieving, it's
the girl I met. We were so happy.'

I know. I saw them together. It was a whirlwind of
passion, tender moments and the look I haven't seen on
his face since—well, we met all those years ago. He lost her.
And we lost our dreams. Love with that depth doesn't strike
every day, every month or every year.

He speaks of her. Of memories. Of what-ifs. Of his confusion. I try my best not to think guiltily about my own lover,
my other significant other, sleeping in the bedroom. This
heartbreak is his alone. And I am the lucky one.

But I miss her too. We are still friends, supposedly.
And yet everything has changed. She's not coming over
every other day. Her laughter doesn't sound in the kitchen
anymore. We have no exotic perfume traces on the sofa, the

bedsheets or my clothes that she tried on and were three sizes too big for her. I miss her smell. After two months, it's all been scrubbed away through the normal wear and tear of life. I listen to the playlist they created on Spotify, when they were still in love. 'Addicted' by Avicii. 'Happy' by Pharrell Williams. 'I've Got You' by Marc Anthony, the last of the great romantics in company with my boyfriend. I wonder how many times he's listened to it. How many times they made love to it.

And I cry for him.

It would be easy to play the drama triangle. To see her as the girl who trampled on him. But that's not how it happened and besides, it does no good to think that way. It only heaps the burning coals onto a situation that's painful enough.

I don't blame her for her change in heart even in the moments that I see my boyfriend lost and unhappy. Our lifestyle is, after all, difficult... extraordinarily joyous but comes with a heavy dose of rejection from society. Was it that which made her heart switch off? Was it the realisation that she was monogamous after all? Even she didn't really know.

So she left. We plotted and we planned in the height of summer, and we were all the unhappier because the world was so glorious. Because when you've broken up with someone, there's a hole that's left behind. And all you want to do is fill it. The response from those who didn't understand was, 'Cheer up, you've still got one girlfriend left.'

But the hole in his heart was shaped like her and only she fitted in it. I didn't. That hole, that wound had to heal.

It was bleeding and I didn't have tissues big enough to clean up the mess.

Then a month later he said, 'I guess I'll throw her tooth-brush away then.'

And I nodded in reply, breathing in relief and sadness. It was over, and she wasn't coming back.

The child I cannot claim

Jessica Burde

She is not my child.

I have told her bedtime stories, until I had no more tales.
I taught her of why flowers die, and why the seasons
change.

She is not my child.

She calls me 'Ima'—mommy—and holds my hand.
She told me, 'that's alright then, you always keep
your promises.'

She is not my child.

Just my children's stepsister, my ex's stepdaughter.
Just the daughter of my heart, and the trusting
    hand in mine.

She is not my child.

The court does not care that she calls me Ima.
The court does not see that they take her from me also.

She is not my child.

I have no rights, no voice, no hope.
No reason, they say, to grieve.

But she is my child.

I have said the blessing over her each shabbas,
and taught her the sacred prayers.

She is my child.

I have tucked her in at night,
and held her while she cried.

She is my child.

And as much as the courts take her from her mother,
The mother I was not even allowed to speak for

They take her from me.

Polyculous bonds

Julie Fennell

I was born in 1981, and grew up in the shadow of AIDS and an era of "love can kill you" rhetoric. The messages were simultaneously decisive—"sexually transmitted infections (STIs) are shameful, dangerous, painful, and gross"—and vague—"you can get them from basically any sexual contact, but only sluts get them." To further underscore our risk, we were constantly reminded that in terms of our disease risk, we not only had sex with Joe—we had sex with everyone Joe had ever had sex with as well (as if condoms were irrelevant in these calculations). The sexual miseducation of my generation was well encapsulated in a brilliant segment in the movie *Mean Girls* (2004), where a health education teacher writes "klamydia" on the board, instructing his adolescent pupils, "If you touch each other, you will get chlamydia ... and die," then further warns, "Don't have sex, because you will get pregnant and die!" and concludes by passing out a bowl of condoms.

As a professional sociologist, I have long been fascinated by the effect this kind of rhetoric has had on people's contraceptive attitudes and behavior. My dissertation research in 2006 focused on the way that (mostly monogamous) heterosexual Americans made decisions about contraceptive use. I found that some people took the threat of STIs and unintended pregnancy very seriously, and others were aware of the risks but didn't seem particularly concerned about those risks for themselves. I was somewhat dismayed to find that, at that time at least, most of the people who had extensive histories of casual sex were the ones who took those risks the least seriously. Meanwhile, most of the people who had the least to worry about in terms of actual STI risk were the ones who had usually been the most conscientious condom users. Clearly, the intended social message about sexual risk had penetrated the heterosexual population on the whole in a perverse fashion.

I have been immersed in the polyamorous subculture now for nearly six years, and it has been both my personal experience and my professional observation that unlike monogamous people having casual sex, cultural messages about sexual risks have made deep and lasting impressions among poly folk. As frightening as it might be to think that you are having sex with everyone Joe has ever had sex with, imagine the added fear of regularly coming face-to-face with the four or five people that Joe is *currently* having sex with. In a world where "love can kill," polyamory sounds extravagantly dangerous. Rather than becoming callous, most polyamorous people—especially those who, like me, also self-identify as "polysexual" and have often tried to reclaim the label "slut" as an identity—tend to be extremely fearful of STIs. Poly folks often (vastly) overestimate their statistical risk for contracting STIs, and use condoms with the attitude of religious zealots.

Fear of STIs is generally so high, and functional role models are often so few, that I have taken to describing the situation of *fluid-bonding* among poly people as *anomic.* (*Anomic* is a fancy French sociological word that means that people aren't really sure what the rules are for a particular situation, and that that uncertainty often causes anxiety, discord, and/or guilt). Indeed, polyamorous people can't often agree on what the term "fluid-bonded" (or "fluid-bound") even means: the general consensus seems to be that fluid-bonded partners are partners who have penis-in-vagina (PIV) and/or penis-in-anus (PIA) sex without condoms. Afraid of stigma, diseases, and the rapid spread of these between partners, the polyamorous subculture tends to discourage people from having unpro-tected sex, and provides little guidance for the structuring of safe fluid-bonded poly groups. In a context of serious sexual risk, how can a person safely become fluid-bonded with more than one person?

The answer to that question in Poly World, as it is in Mono World, is trust. People have to decide what diseases they're most concerned about and trust that their partners and (this is the really hard one) their partners' partners will follow their safer sex agreements. On the other hand, the nature of poly life can sometimes ameliorate anxieties. As intimidating as it may be to regularly come face to face with your partner's partners and see your cumulative sexual health risk right before your eyes, there is a certain comfort to it as well, in part because it gives you a much clearer idea of what's going on. I'm not saying that poly people never cheat on each other, but they usually have a lot less motivation to do so. It's not too hard to trust that your husband will use condoms with his fuck buddy when the two of them have sex in your bedroom and know you could accidentally walk in on them at any moment (or deliberately walk in and join them!). And if you and your husband's girlfriend are hooking up with the same guy, it's a lot easier to trust that she's using condoms with him too ... And this is the way that my partners and I live.

The five of us started calling ourselves a "polycule" back in the fall of 2012, when our relationships and sexual lives were so thoroughly entangled with one another that we looked like several relationship atoms often sharing orbits together. Our self-described polycule was habitually having orgies together (I'm changing the names to protect the not-so-innocent here): me and my husband, Jonny; his girlfriend, Theresa; my boyfriend Grant, who was also hooking up with Theresa; and my girlfriend Amy, who was in a triadic relationship with me and Grant, and who was occasionally hooking up with Jonny. At that point, those relationships formed the core of our serious dynamics (although we all still occasionally slept with other people as well). Jonny and I were fluid-bonded and had been for many years; Jonny and Theresa were already fluid-bonded, which functionally meant that Theresa and I were fluid-bonded through him; and Amy and Grant became fluid-bonded during that fall. And so the question became: did Jonny, Theresa, and I want to become fluid-bonded to Amy and Grant?

After much discussion, we decided the answer was yes. We were all a little bit nervous about each other's tendencies to have sex with other people, but we were comforted by the fact that we were mostly sleeping with each other's fuck buddies anyway (sometimes in tandem). Our social and sexual worlds were quite thoroughly overlapped, and that really meant that whatever risks one of us faced, all the others faced anyway. So we decided, in the sexiest and most entertaining way possible, to create a "fluid-bound contract." The goal was to create a set of rules so easy to follow that even someone who was thoroughly intoxicated should be able to keep to them. The rules we developed were as follows:

§ The "polycule" defined here consists of a fluid-bound group of [partners list].

§ For the purposes described here, "fluid-bonding" includes functionally all bodily fluids, both sexual and non-sexual.

§ All anal and vaginal intercourse outside the polycule should be protected with barriers.

§ All members of the polycule should keep an updated list of people outside of the polycule that they define as "current partners" in a shared Google document.

§ All members of the polycule should email the shared Google group whenever they have anything that could reasonably be defined as sex with someone who is not on their list of "current partners" or in the polycule.

§ Any sexual partners of anyone outside the polycule should be aware that anyone within it might ask them about their current testing status and their current partners. And they should be happy about this because it means we value each other's safety!

§ If a condom breaks or goes amiss during intercourse with anyone outside the polycule, it should be immediately reported to all members of the polycule, as should the outside partner's current testing status, so that subsequent fluid-bonding can be re-evaluated.

§ If an unintentional blood-based fluid-exchange occurs, it should be immediately reported to all members of the polycule for subsequent fluid-bonding re-evaluation.

§ The polycule will try to schedule a once-a-month group processing session. If there is nothing to discuss, then we will try to watch a movie together. All processing sessions are to conclude in sex.

§ This polycule is not defined as "polyfidelitous"; however, there is an expectation that members will be limiting intercourse with people outside the polycule.

§ Members are expected to get screened for STIs at least once every six months and to check on the testing statuses of any partners outside the polycule.

§ This agreement will be re-evaluated and re-negotiated after [date], pending the preferences of all involved, with the default assumption that it will dissolve at that time.

Rather than simply writing it all out on a piece of paper and signing it, we took a more fun-loving approach. I wrote the important points of the contract onto Theresa's body with Sharpie pens, and then we all signed her ass and took pictures of it (we also had a more conventional typewritten contract as well). We posted our contract to the social networking website of our community, both so our friends could provide social support for what we were doing, and to increase our own accountability in holding to it. And it worked. Many people told us how interested they were in what we were doing, and how they thought it was cool that we had been willing to go public with something that so many poly people hide under a rug (we were having a lot of sex in public, so we figured we were probably better off being public about it). Again and again, people asked me what were the greatest challenges of maintaining such an arrangement; I told them honestly that the challenges had absolutely nothing to do with the fluid-bonding, and everything to do with the complexities of managing so many very different relationships.

The hardest thing about "polyculous" dynamics—which is to say, highly overlapped and interlocking relationship patterns, as opposed to more standard poly relationship Anna-Brad-Cathy-Drake chains—is that different relationships are both physically and metaphorically all over each other. Poly life always has the hazard of relationship stresses and (successes) bleeding into each other, even in chain dynamics. But in polyculous dynamics, regardless of fluid-bonding, everything starts to get a lot stickier. We were around each other enough that we all ended up judging each other's relationships a lot. Our relationships were sufficiently entangled that it was sometimes difficult to figure out what each of them signified. Even more confusing was the fact that relationship dynamics amongst our polyculous members started shifting before the contract was even signed. Several months in, we realized that not everyone really seemed to agree on what our lovingly crafted contract really *meant*: how connected was everyone really going to be? In particular, we couldn't escape the fact that fluid-bonding is normally a symbol of serious romantic attachment, though several of our poly-culous members were now fluid-bonded and occasion-ally having sex, but not in romantic relationships with each other.

Things worked really well between us for about six months (three months before we signed the contract, and for about three months after), and then our various issues starting weighing on us more heavily. We tried to "resolve" a lot of our issues by spending less time together as a group and disentangling our relationships more, but we lost a sense of group connectedness as a result. After about six months, we were still more closely bonded than many poly groups, but our polyculous identity was greatly diminished. After a couple of years, some of the relation-ships petered out, and I was left married to Jonny, Jonny was still in a relationship with Theresa, and Amy was still in a relationship with Grant.

I suppose to many people reading this, my story sounds like the cautionary tale of a failed experiment. But I don't think that any of us approached this arrangement naively. We were all experienced polyamorists, and we knew that the more complex the relationship dynamics, the harder they are to juggle. We juggled impressively for months, but we started dropping balls along the way. People in our community seemed to assume that the fluid-bonding would be our biggest challenge, but it never was. I never stopped trusting my partners or feeling safe with them. But our romantic relationships changed, and that's okay. All relationships shift and change, and it doesn't mean that they "failed." It's why I wrote the contract to default to end at a particular date, so that we had to actively decide to renew it every few months. When we finally decided to close it out, we all had dinner together, and all agreed that we would all remain friends and occasional sexual partners, but just not remain a large fluid-bound group anymore. Our polycule has divided back into (slightly altered) relationship atoms.

Love hasn't killed us. At least, not yet.

Monogamish musings
Marla Renee Stewart

Although I dated throughout high school, I didn't really start seriously dating until I was in college. For me, I defined dating as going out with various people and having the opportunity to make out with them, have sex with them and go out to different events with them. I reveled in the fact that I was always open about who else I was dating. People often seem shocked that I would reveal the fact that I was dating someone else besides them, but they always went along with it. Most of them didn't date anyone else but me, and I didn't seem to mind. Besides, I liked the attention.

My freshman year in college, I dated a constantly drunk baseball player, a woman's basketball player (I was also on the team) and flirted with numerous others as I continued on my journey to self-discovery. I came out as bisexual in high school, so dating women and men felt comfortable for me and easy. I was a pretty good flirt and got what I wanted most of the time, so dating came easily.

I continued to date throughout college and got into a few serious relationships (I was in college for six years). During this time when I was attending college at San Francisco State, I studied human sexuality and LGBT studies. People came to me all the time with their sex questions and took my advice, and I educated people constantly about sex and sexuality.

Because I was a knowledge junkie, I learned about polyamory and what it was, and even had a few friends who were polyamorous. Although it completely made sense to me, I didn't identify as poly, and I'm not sure why. I dated multiple people, so it wouldn't be so far-fetched to fall in love with different people. But it didn't resonate then, and it doesn't resonate now. However, it's not like I didn't try. ;)

As a sex and sexuality educator, I felt that it was only fair to always experiment with my sexuality. When my girlfriend at the time and I moved out to Atlanta, we had fun in our relationship, but I noticed that I wanted something more that I wasn't getting from our monogamous relationship. We had decided to open up our relationship (she had had previous experiences with open relationships) and we navigated it successfully, but I felt that wasn't what I was looking for.

My next relationship started open, as we were temporarily relating long distance. However, I found myself being jealous when she shared with me about having sex with another woman. I'm not a jealous person, so this feeling felt awful. After she moved here, we settled on rules that worked for the both of us. Our main rule was that we could have sex with other people if both of us were involved. This worked for us completely! This felt right to me. I even told my parents that I was a non-monogamous person. They just marked it up as another one of my quirks. I love my parents.

Regardless, I had the comfort of monogamy while being open to expressing myself sexually with other people. A perfect match for me.

However, it wasn't a perfect match for my girlfriend. She wanted more. I was working seventy-hour weeks, compared to her twenty, and her free time needed to be occupied. I occasionally gave her little projects to do for me here and there, but soon enough, she was engaging with a couple of other women and one woman in particular took a liking to the both of us.

We hung out a lot and she spent the night a lot and her relationship with each of us was different and amazing. Until it wasn't for me. I realized that I couldn't stand her personal drama. And it's not because it was hers—I believe it was my inability to have the capacity to deal with my own stuff, my partner's stuff and her stuff as well. As a natural healer and problem solver, I wanted to help her with her problems, but in my head, I just felt that she was making stupid decisions, one after another, and I'm not a fan of someone who doesn't learn from their mistakes.

Although we found ourselves in this hanging triangle (she had another partner), I was tired. I didn't want it anymore. In fact, I realized that I didn't want to be with my girlfriend anymore either. After a while, we had a "don't ask, don't tell" policy that mainly pertained to her because I was working non-stop trying to get my company off the ground. I wasn't having sex with anyone else and I was ready to be a full-fledged entrepreneur. So I broke up with her.

I remained single for almost a year, dating a couple of people and having fun. I ended up dating this guy and we had a really rocky start. He assured me that I should be comfortable to express to him when I have the desires to be with women (I had already told him that I would need to have sex with women during our relationship). However,

187

when we became more serious, he became crass when I expressed to him how much I missed being with women. I found myself not knowing how to approach the situation and feeling like I couldn't express how I truly felt because I didn't want the repercussions of what he might say to me. Overall, it wasn't worth the additional stress. When I told him that I believed in polyamory theoretically, but will not practice it, he just about lost his mind. I think he wanted me to be something I wasn't and when I mentioned something I was that he didn't like, he fought with me about it. It was his first time being with an actively queer woman and being that he was from the Democratic Republic of Congo and I was from liberal northern California, our belief systems were dramatically different. But that's a whole 'nother story.

After being engaged to him and then breaking up with him (for a whole slew of reasons), I realized that I didn't want to sacrifice my sexuality for anyone.

My single life has allowed me to do more soul-searching, reflect on my past successes and mistakes, and approach every person that I'm talking to or dating with integrity and reflective honesty. I've realized that the strict definitions of monogamy don't work for me. However, being monogamish does work for me. The ability to be completely open with my partner and express my feelings without them feeling jealous would be heaven for me. As a person who revels in compersion, I would love for my partner to be the same. My ideal lifestyle would be one emotional connection and multiple sexual connections occasionally. My ideal lifestyle is monogamish and I will have nothing less.

Some people just know things. Some people just practice things. Some people have to practice things to know things. I knew things about myself. I learned more things by getting out of my comfort zone and practicing things. From that practice, I learned new things and relearned things that I already knew.

And those are my monogamish musings...

Polyamory round trip
Baldwin Omni

I was introduced to the concept of an "open relationship" in early 1969 at age 19, although the term "polyamory" was not coined until 1990. The office manager where I worked, a man age 39, was trying to convince me to go back and finish college. One day at lunch, he smiled and asked me, "How's your sex life?" I replied, "What sex life?" Little did I know what would ensue. He invited me over to his home for dinner and to go over possible paths, got me slightly inebriated, and said instead of driving under the influence I should sleep on their hide-a-bed sofa in the living room. I'm trying to fall asleep, when suddenly there's a beautiful woman—tall, slender, fit, and age 37—standing next to the sofa, completely naked, smiling and saying, "Having trouble sleeping? Perhaps I can help." Oh, did she ever help . . . Her husband explained over breakfast that they had an open relationship. She had a steady boyfriend in addition to her husband, and he had a girlfriend. I had the opportunity for several more "tutoring sessions" before they moved out of the area for better jobs.

At age 22, a female friend invited me to attend a swinging party. Physically, it was delightful, but I wondered why it "didn't feel quite right" emotionally.

I got engaged at age 24. My fiancée and I were talking about what we wanted our marriage to be like. She said (before I could bring up the topic) that she wanted an open marriage, where we could have emotional and physical connections to others if we wished, with the other knowing and consenting beforehand. She suggested we leave "forsaking all others" out of the vows we wrote, since she didn't feel it was realistic. We both did have other partners— mostly people who were already my, her, or our friends. I had told her about the few swinging parties I'd attended before we met. She expressed curiosity—and ended up attending a number of parties with me, and enjoying it.

In 1980, my wife had a dramatic transformation in her faith, and got very involved in a conservative Christian church. She said she didn't want to "do this anymore, it's wrong." Out of respect for her, I also ceased any outside activities—for 26 years.

In 2006, after seeing *Merry Wives of Windsor* with the theme of Falstaff's infidelities and their consequences, my wife initiated an extraordinary conversation. She thanked me for decades of faithful, loving partnership, and said she felt guilty that I wasn't being true to myself all those years due to a misunderstanding which she neglected to correct—that she changed, but didn't expect me to change. She offered me a "Don't Ask, Don't Tell" (DADT) situation. I found this very difficult—it felt completely wrong to me not being able to honestly tell her what I might be doing. In early 2007, I met a couple who had just been to a poly workshop. They wanted to try opening their marriage. She and I began a relationship. My wife consented to my doing this. (I later found out she thought it was just a mid-life crisis where I wanted to sow some wild oats. She assumed it was all about sex, and never considered that there might be an emotional component.)

I found out why swinging hadn't felt right. I wasn't seeking a lot of recreational sex; rather, I wanted someone with whom I could have an emotional bond, and that was more important than the sex alone. I realized I'd always been poly and not known it.

The husband started being possessive and jealous. He wasn't ready for poly. Also, his wife and I found that he thought "poly" would be a way for him to get sex with more women, without guilt. He was seeking to be a swinger, not poly, and found it very difficult to accept that his wife had entered into a second emotional bond.

She and I quickly decided to stop being lovers. Both are still my very good friends.

What ensued over the next several years, while I was still married and living with a very monogamous spouse, was a series of relationships where I was a secondary or tertiary partner to the "other woman." One lived with the father of her six-year-old child (not married), and had a long-term primary-equivalent partner as well. Another lived in a "vee" or polyaffective relationship with two straight men, and so on. I wasn't getting enough companionship and affection at home. Neither my wife nor I wanted to go through the trauma of a divorce, so we just "continued to continue." I wasn't getting enough companionship, affection, and quality time from the outside relationships either, not much sex, and a lot of stress. Eventually my wife and I separated and divorced. We were simply moving in quite different directions in our lives. She asked, "What do you do when the circles on the MasterCard logo no longer overlap?"

My psychologist believes that my ex-wife offering me more freedom and subsequently accepting poly was simply "setting me up"—giving me more than enough rope to hang myself. She portrayed herself as the innocent victim of a philanderer having a mid-life "itch." This let her look blameless to our adult children, her friends, and her family. I took the high road, and would not tell the kids that Mom wasn't telling the full truth. It's been difficult. I hope eventually the kids and I can reconcile.

In October 2011, I met a woman who said that she and her husband were poly, and it was ok if she began a relationship with me. Between her house, husband, and two school-age kids, there was a limited amount of time available for us to spend together. It turned out that she and her husband had each briefly dated someone years before, but they never became full relationships. Also, we found that her husband only expected she would date and have sex with someone else, not get emotionally involved and threaten his exclusivity. After a couple of months, he said he wanted a divorce. Had she understood his position and conveyed it to me up front, I wouldn't have moved forward. They ended up getting counseling and remaining together. He and I actually became friends, and I became like a surrogate dad to the kids. On a number of occasions, the entire family would come to my home for dinner and perhaps a movie, then the husband would take the kids home while she stayed overnight. The young daughter sometimes smiled and asked if Mommy was having a sleepover at my house.

Again, I didn't have enough companionship, touch, and quality time. I was lonely and depressed. Things got markedly worse when she met someone else and suddenly had flaming NRE (New Relationship Energy) with him. I felt I was in his shadow. She reworked the shared calendar, and my "date time" with her got cut in half so that he could have time too. Trying to juggle three relationships plus kids plus house had her overloaded. I tried to tell her that what she was doing terrified me, since several previous partners had met someone new and left me for them. I thought that was happening again. She didn't understand. Our relationship rapidly went downhill and ended badly. Very badly. I had been like a substitute parent to her preteen children, and not being able to continue interacting with the kids I loved hurt me a great deal. She admitted that this was a classic case of "relationship broken, add another person" on her part, that I was trying to have something that wasn't available, a primary relationship, and she was trying to rescue a dysfunctional marriage. Neither was healthy.

Looking back on my attempts at poly relationships, I realized that my needs had not been met being a secondary or less, and that the only way poly would work for me was if I had a stable healthy primary relationship where we had one or more secondary relationships. Very sadly, I realized that I'd been starved for warm affection and touch for over 30 years.

My attempts at finding someone poly who might possibly become a primary proved fruitless. I decided to change my online dating profile to not mention poly, and see what happened. Suddenly, I was almost inundated with people viewing my profile and a number of them sending me messages. I started dating, wanting to find out if I could tolerate being monogamous.

I met a woman about my age in February 2014. She had been divorced eight years from an emotionally and occasionally physically abusive marriage.

The good part: we lived only 15 minutes apart, and spent a lot of time together. I finally had someone to simply hang out with, be friends with, and "do stuff" with—picnics, drives, movies (particularly nice: movies at my house where she liked to hold hands and lean against my shoulder on the couch), and games (Scrabble, backgammon, etc.). I felt vastly more peaceful, content, and productive. We talked and text messaged every day. I felt like I had a warm, smiling affectionate friend, companion, and sweetheart. And four generations of her family liked me.

The bad news: her ex-husband left her with a steamer trunk of baggage. It took a long time for her to gradually open up to emotional and physical intimacy. She realized I was respecting her and being very patient, and that helped a great deal. So, for that time period, I basically gave up intercourse, and committed to being monogamous with her unless we decided it couldn't work and broke up.

I was happier having this warm connection with her than I was in relationships where there wasn't this kind of emotional link. I found that the smiles, affection, and time together mattered more to me than sex (although I hoped to have both). I felt that over time, she would realize just how different I was from her ex, and things between us would only improve. We planned two vacation trips: six nights at Reno/Tahoe, and a week in Arizona.

The six-day vacation ended after two days. We drove back in silence. I dropped her at her house, and we never spoke again. I let my hope and optimism mask the communications issues and, in my opinion, her serious OCD and other neuroses. It simply couldn't have worked.

Just before Thanksgiving 2014, a woman messaged me on a dating site. We chatted online, then on the phone. Then we met for lunch, and after that for dinner. We both felt right away that we were friends, with potential for more. The "more" quickly developed. Both she and I had prior marriages of more than 30 years, neither of which satisfied us emotionally or sexually. I feel at home with her, and she with me. My psychologist remarked that he's never seen me this peaceful and happy. We don't want to rush into anything, but so far it seems to both of us that each of us considers the other "the one." She commented that we feel like soul mates who were pre-destined to meet. We just returned from a week's vacation out of state, which was delightful. I've been almost living at her home, going back to my house one or two days a week to get the mail, water the plants, do a few chores. We're gradually moving towards more balance, with perhaps four nights a week at her home and three nights apart. It would be difficult for her to sleep over at my house due to an elderly mother who lives with her. That's ok for now. We both realize we need some time to be individuals. Distance is also an issue, as we live about 80 miles apart.

Could I be poly again? Possibly, under the right circumstances. However, my current partner only wants a monogamous relationship. I'm feeling that monogamy will work, provided the relationship continues to grow emotionally, and it continues to include mutually satisfying sex. Whether I'm comfortably settling into a one-on-one relationship because more of my needs as a person are being met than ever before, or because my flirtations with poly were from within a less-than-fulfilling marriage, I can't say. My current feeling is that poly simply didn't meet my needs, and caused a lot of pain.

I know a few poly households where it seems to be working. I know more where it didn't work. Perhaps my forays into poly when things weren't great at home were cases of "relationship broken, add more people." Perhaps I simply got involved with the wrong people or for the wrong reasons. I don't know. I do know that at present I'm happier than I've ever been…

Part V: For the long haul

Happily triadic

Cascade Spring Cook and
Zhahai Spring Stewart

We (Cascade and Zhahai) have lived together for almost 40 years. We have had our own evolving flavor of polyamorous relationship for the whole time, in that we did not base our relationship on a promise of monogamy and we were selectively open to other possibilities—and for most of that time, one or both of us have had other lovers.

Four years ago we embarked on a new adventure. We chose a house where we could include an additional person, our sweetie John. We have had decades to create and refine our own patterns of living together well as a twosome (we've also never had kids). How was a three-adult household going to work—especially with an emotionally close friend and lover?

Six years earlier, we had moved across the country to live closer to good friends, groups we were involved with, and a lover that Zhahai was very close to, Laurie. She was married and living with her husband (also polyamorous). Shortly after we moved, Cascade became involved with John—the man who was now going to live with us.

By the time we were looking for a house, Cascade had become very close to John, and Zhahai and John were good friends. We knew that John was tired of living alone—he had long desired to live in a community. So we decided to seek a house where John could live with us.

After much searching we finally found the right house—a rare house in our town—with an "in-law" unit for John which connects to the rest of the house through an inside door—so it's easy to walk back and forth, but John still has his distinct living space with privacy and acoustic isolation when that door is closed.

We bought the house using equity and credit-worthiness we've accumulated over our decades together, and we are responsible for the mortgage. John pays rent/a share of house and food expenses. We felt it was best not to entangle our differing finances (and financial styles), and that seems to have been a good idea.

SHARING THE HOUSEHOLD

John has his own living room and kitchen (though he uses the latter only lightly, as we usually eat dinners together in the main house). One advantage of having this distinct space has been to allow John to have his own house-keeping standards.

All of us struggle with clutter and organization, and it has been helpful to decouple our cycles of order and disorder from John's cycles, so we don't feel a need to pressure each other to match (this is enough of an issue just between us; we've achieved a mostly harmonious approach that nevertheless stretches our tolerance at times—and adding a third person would tend to raise the complexity of this balancing act).

It turned out that the ability to close the door to the in-law apartment for acoustic isolation was also very important—we had not realized that John almost always has the TV on or a movie playing when he's in his living room or study area. This would drive us batty if it was in our living space, and it would frustrate him if he had to live by our preferences. It's also handy for John to be able to set his own thermostat and to keep his own hours (he's often up late).

We share a bedroom, where we sleep most nights, and John sleeps in his bedroom in the in-law apartment. The two of us typically have a "date night" every week when we put aside our busy-ness and focus on each other. We also typically have another "date night" each week when Cascade sleeps with John in his bedroom, and Zhahai sleeps with Laurie in our bedroom (Laurie's home is not a good place for Zhahai and Laurie to spend the night).

Often the four of us will have dinner together on a date night—John and Laurie are good friends too, but not lovers. For holiday meals and other gatherings this group of four increases to six with Laurie's husband and his other lover as well—making another level of family.

Occasionally we have a three-way date with just John, and the three of us sleep together in our bed, which is the only king-size bed in the house. This has been loving and erotic for all of us, and has probably helped us bond and enjoy each other.

On a practical level, none of us sleep quite as well in the middle, so we figure out each time who gets that position—usually not Zhahai since he's a furnace. Sometimes it can work well to have two blankets with the middle person having a choice of which blanket to share—and can also get some cooling air.

ABOUT THE DYNAMICS

Our desire is for deep, passionate connection—not just sex and light friendship. We also tend towards ongoing connections with a few close intimates. John has now been in our lives for 10 years, and Laurie for 14 years. We expect to live with John, and that Zhahai will be lovers with Laurie, for the rest of our lives.

The three of us living together (John and us) are very supportive of each other, in various combinations. Zhahai has given John good advice on "the care and feeding of Cascade" when John and Cascade are having a conflict or disconnect. Zhahai tries to gently talk with Cascade if he observes her being sharp with John. And John has supported each of us when we have some tension. John and Zhahai have not had much conflict, but Cascade is available for any support they need.

Some people have the idea that everyone in this type of "living together as more than friends" relationship "should" be equal. That's great for some people, but it's not what works for us. We are married, share finances, and spend the most time together—and while John is also very close and deeply connected to both of us, it's not quite at the same level.

That probably wouldn't work if John tended to compare his relationships with us to our relationship with each other and feel bad. Instead he tends to compare his life within our variety of threesome to the other relationships he has had over the decades, and to be very appreciative of what we three have created together—in particular his relationship with Cascade, but also the intimacy with Zhahai. He is also pretty independent, and has lived alone more than with a partner.

We got into polyamory long ago (before the term was coined) with the understanding that we really valued our relationship and intended not to let loving others disrupt our closeness. At the same time, we can have deep, loving connections with others, relationships with their own integrity. This combination has required some careful balancing, where everybody's feelings and needs matter, and it's also true that we have priorities.

The relationship with John has been very compatible with our commitment to each other, as he truly respects and honors the relationship we have built over the decades, and would not want to do anything to undermine it. That in turn allows us to love him more and more, as we do.

We don't want to integrate finances with John beyond sharing expenses like food and house-related expenses. For more than a decade, we kept our own finances somewhat separate; that way we didn't get as much into the trap of fighting about finances. By now we have merged our finances, and we have similar values about spending and saving money. John has his own monetary style which differs from ours, so by keeping separate finances we each get freedom to choose our own balance without needing an elusive consensus.

John also has other lovers, though not as intense as the relationship with us. We're also good friends with his lovers, who tend to socialize some with us when they visit him.

CHALLENGES

While things work very well overall in sharing the household with John, there was some initial discomfort in adjusting to another person—there are some positives and some negatives, as one might expect.

Zhahai: There was a period in the early months of the new expanded household when it really sunk in more deeply that this was not just an "experiment" where we'd see how it goes and play it by ear—like living in a group household in college. Instead John was very likely to live with us, with the compromises and changes that involves, for the rest of our lives. If it turned out to not quite work well for me (without being disastrous), it would be extremely painful and difficult to "kick John out," so I felt trapped.

I was feeling like I enjoyed seeing more of John than previously, but maybe not quite as much as was happening, which was a major increase. We were able to talk about that, and I did feel heard. We've continued to work on that balance, in a mutually caring way.

In practice, for us there is an ongoing element involved of consciously focusing more on the positive and on appreciating and enjoying what works, rather than drifting into excessive focus on the negatives. That approach is related to how we have learned to connect so well with each other, and be more at ease in the world in general; and in all cases it does take some mindfulness rather than just running on autopilot.

However that only works for us if we also can talk about any problems or feelings, so it's based on choosing a good mental state, but not on suppressing real issues. And the three of us have been doing well at that—hearing each other and caring about each other and looking for win-win approaches that take everybody's needs into consideration.

So we wouldn't say it doesn't take any effort to make things work, but it's a good kind of effort that also helps us grow and open up, not a grim determination or self-delusion. If we were not fairly good at that balance, we would not have managed to have such an intimate and rewarding relationship with each other over the decades. The same skills have worked well with John, who did not communicate so powerfully with his earlier partners, but eagerly learned to communicate very well in our expanded relationship.

Cascade: One of the things I've really appreciated about John is that when I've told him "We need to talk," he has responded very well. Instead of running away like many men do, he consciously frames it as my expressing a desire to be closer to him. So he has always listened well and we find a way to resolve the issue that is bothering me.

One area where we haven't yet found our course is vacation, and traveling in particular, because the time for that is a scarcity in our current lives. Our trips together have always been important to us and we travel well together, but in recent years we feel like we haven't been having enough time for that—so it's hard to also find much time for three-way vacations (which do not fulfill quite the same need), and for John and Cascade alone. Perhaps we can sort that out better when we retire, health permitting. This hasn't been a source of friction for us because we know that we all care about each other, but we are aware that it's an area where it's harder to meet everybody's desires (which is what we try to do).

A more recent challenge is that Cascade has taken another lover, whom she sees much less often but with whom she nevertheless has a deep and growing relation-ship. He'd love to have more time with her but respects her existing relationships. Zhahai likes the other man and they connect well, but he has an ongoing concern that another substantial relationship may rock the boat or make it harder to find the right balance to meet everybody's needs. Zhahai is concerned not just about his quality time with Cascade, and her own already full plate in keeping up with life's demands, but also wants to be sure that Cascade and John have enough time and energy together. Zhahai and Laurie also have an ongoing and meaningful relationship with another woman, but Zhahai does not think that's as much of a challenge, because it's less intense.

REWARDS

We have learned a lot over the years about accepting each other as we are—partly through doing our own work and attending workshops, and partly with the help of others in our lives. Each of us has learned a lot from relationships with other lovers. In particular, Cascade learned that she doesn't have to be bugged by certain things Zhahai does by noticing that she doesn't react the same way when someone else—like John—is doing something similar.

Zhahai: I used to become reactive or withdrawn when Cascade became sharp or critical, but from observing Cascade with John, I learned that she could often pull herself out of that mode more quickly if I could react less.

Cascade: I've learned to express my feelings as simply feelings—and not blame anyone for them. I've learned to let Zhahai have his feelings. I can listen and allow change to happen within myself, but I don't have to try to fix anything, or shut him down. We believe that truly listening means allowing oneself to possibly be changed by what we hear, which is different than being controlled by what somebody wants, and also different than "listening" as a technique for managing others.

We've also had the pleasure of living and loving with our sweetheart, John. The three of us talk around the dinner table, work on projects together, watch movies. There is a lot of love and affection in the household—and laughter. We have wonderful erotic times together. As mentioned earlier, we all support each other emotionally in many combinations. In general, the good things we had hoped for in moving in together have indeed come to pass.

And how has it been for John? We'll let him speak for himself on that.

John: I had been in a polyamorous relationship prior to meeting Cascade, but my former partner tended to be over-controlling and hypercritical of me. My relationship with Cascade was refreshing because she gave me positive reinforcement and listened to me. I appreciated her bond with Zhahai and made the commitment early on to be supportive of their relationship. My developing friendship with Zhahai was an important element here. Cascade and I had been lovers for over six years when she and Zhahai invited me to share their new home. Having my own space while sharing meals, movies, etc., was a good fit for me, since I value my privacy and independence (Cascade and Zhahai also have private offices). At first Zhahai expressed some uneasiness about the new arrangement, but he could see that I respected his needs and wanted to make things work. We all have found that honest, empathetic communication allows us to work through any bumps in the road to achieve good outcomes, and our mutual relationship continues to deepen as a result.

Fortifying the pillars of our house
TammyJo Eckhart, PhD

When my husband, Tom, and I were married in 1992 we wrote our own vows and we didn't say anything about monogamy. In fact, we used the third chapter of *The Prophet* by Kahlil Gibran, a chapter about marriage, as one of our readings to reflect our hopes and wishes for our future together. For those of you not familiar with this part of the poem, please consider it now.

> Give your hearts, but not into each other's keeping.
> For only the hand of Life can contain your hearts.
> And stand together, yet not too near together:
> For the pillars of the temple stand apart,
> And the oak tree and the cypress grow not in each other's shadow.

While the poem shares a good deal with our philosophy, it isn't perfect. We fully believe that we need to be individual people, that we can't rely upon each other for happiness or fulfillment, but must find that within ourselves, with each other, or with others. We fully believe that each of us needs to become the best person s/he can become by working within and without, with each other, and with others. We fully believe that our uniqueness needs to be nurtured by self, each other, and with others. We fully believe that our commonalities need to be celebrated by self, each other, and with others. We are the pillars that hold our family up, that raise us above the tremors or shelter us from the storms that life throws our way.

This "with others" is the reason we didn't include vows about monogamy in our wedding. I'd love to say that we planned being poly from the start, but that wouldn't be honest, and what we did promise was to be honest with each other and with ourselves. We didn't make a pledge about monogamy because it didn't seem important to either of us. If we loved each other, if we took our plan to be married and create a family, then we'd put in the work to make it happen and help it function. Other people, or lack thereof, couldn't weaken the pillars that helped hold up our family unless they were already weak to begin with.

Our rules of being a poly family—we've always felt we were more family than couple—developed over time, at first with trial and error, then seeking advice from other poly folks or watching them succeed (or, more often, fail), and later by doing a lot of reading and talking together. Over time Tom and I developed a set of seemingly simple rules for being poly, rules that still guide us today.

We are honest about what and who we are interested in before we make a move toward a romantic or sexual relationship with that person. This can be a bit tricky, because as you get to know someone it can be easy to go too fast or too far. New relationships are exciting on biological, emotional, and intellectual levels, but we have to value our family enough to stop and remember to communicate our interest within the family before letting things develop too far.

This leads directly to our second rule: we introduce the potential partner to the other(s), and the other(s) need to be honest about their feelings about the person. We do have veto power over potential partners, but in over two decades I can only think of a handful of times we've done this. Why? Using a veto is a shortcut to honest communication. Using a veto is an attempt to strip your partner of their adult power to make choices and can lead to resentment. Using a veto should be the last resort—an action you feel forced to take if you think someone has made a harmful decision.

Normally we'll all meet at a public restaurant and talk; later we'll invite the potential partner to hang out at our house to get to know us, because of our third rule: we are a family. Many poly people we've known over the years are in multiple relationships, most of which barely overlap. Yet while we have done this from time to time, the partners that have lasted longest are those that have become part of our family, adding their pillars to those that support us all. We have a good number of friends who are extended parts of our family, adding their strength from time to time, but not their romantic or sexual energies. If someone wants to become sexual with me, I want the energy we create to nurture the family first and foremost, because I won't do anything to jeopardize the foundation that Tom and I laid.

Our final rule is really a repetition of our wedding vows, to be honest. No matter if a partner has been with us two weeks or twenty years, I expect and need Tom to be honest about how he feels, and he needs me to be honest with him. There are people out there who claim to be poly who aren't, who insist they want to join a family when they don't; these people instead try to break up the existing relationships. It is hard to see that when you are the one infatuated with the new lover, so we need each other to be honest when something seems wrong. Anyone who might join our family needs to understand that Tom and I are the foundations, the main support pillars; we will not be destroyed, and attempts to do so will result in a "don't let the door hit your ass on the way out" reaction. The same applies to all existing relationships. I won't try to break up any of Tom's other partnerships, he won't try to break up mine, and we won't try to break up theirs.

Most of our other partners through the years were short-term, ranging from a couple of months to a year and a half. They spent time with everyone, they considered themselves part of the family, and we consulted with each other about decisions that had to be made. Yet something always came up, like a better job or another relationship that was a better option for the other person. We'd like to think that most of these people left us stronger than when they came in, but again there were bad breakups that made us question our wisdom or even being poly.

Poly isn't a choice for us. It is a reflection of our need to be individuals and to be social, to be loved and to love where we feel empowered. This drive to be more than a couple struggling to be everything to each other feels natural to us. It is not natural to everyone, not even everyone who comes into our family, and this is sometimes why the new pillar just doesn't fit.

Tom and I have been together now since 1992, over two decades, but we are not the sole supports of this family. There is a third pillar in our house and he has been with us since 1999. Fox and I have a D/s (dominant-submissive) dynamic as our foundation. Fox and Tom have a brother-friend connection. The kink isn't new to our family, but the fact that it has lasted this long and become such a strong part of our lives is probably different from many poly families. We don't want to distract you too much by those details, so let us describe how it is different in terms of the rules. All of the same poly rules apply with one slight exception—I do have veto power, and I have used it with Fox because it is my duty as the dominant member to make the final decisions and to foresee any potential problems. Yet I've only used it a few times, because once more the goal of our family is for each of us to become better individuals, and this means empowering each other to do so, not merely enhancing any one individual over the others, kink or not.

Probably the greatest challenge that each of us has had to overcome in this poly family is the rule about being honest. None of us are malicious liars with each other; however, this has been a challenge for each of us in different ways. For Tom it is often a matter of thinking ahead; he's so wrapped up in his own head that he can easily "forget" to tell us about plans and about potential partners. Once he did this to a degree that it crossed our boundaries, and it took us time to recover and caused the loss of the potential relationship, but he seems more cautious of not thinking now. For all of us there have been degrees of hiding the truth from ourselves about what we wanted sexually, how we identified our orientation, or even admitting to events that happened in our lives that deeply affected our development. Two of us grew up hiding things from our families about our sexuality, whether it was simply hiding toys or books or actively creating lies to answer questions.

Lying of any type, for any reason, can damage the trust each member of a family has with the others, so it must be addressed. One way we've done this is through individual and family therapy, where an objective outsider can listen, ask questions, point out problems, and lead us toward solutions. Therapy can become a crutch for doing the work yourself, so we also try to remind each other to express our thoughts and feelings, question inconsistencies, and offer acceptance of the events, behaviors, or desires that were once viewed negatively. Sometimes this results in raised voices or hurt feelings, but primarily we try to just be accepting of each other's uniqueness. If I can't do an activity with Tom because of something from my past, I can still encourage him to go find others who enjoy the same things. If I don't fully understand one part of Fox's identity, I can still buy him gifts that will help him explore it further or role-play out some scenario to help myself comprehend more. The guys might not be able to handle my intensity at all times, but we all know I have options out there, and the guys work to give me time to pursue what I want. Creating an accepting environment reduces the fear that can trigger lying.

One of the challenges society presents to being poly is that you have to manage or juggle multiple relationships, but is that true? If you look at our family today, you see three adults living together and supporting each other. We do this, in part, by following the rules set up in the marriage, but also those of the poly household. Primarily we do this because our type of family offers us more than we feel we'd get as a traditional monogamous couple. In the book Fox and I co-authored, *At Her Feet* (Greenery Press, 2010), we talk a bit about monogamy versus poly and how the basic idea of juggling one relationship or several is misguided. Even in a monogamous couple you have three relationships—self A, self B, and the couple—within the confines of that family. For each new member you add in more and more relationships (2^n-1 of them, to be precise, where n is the number of people). The fact is that the number of relationships holding up your family is the same regardless of whether those people are your kids, your parents, or sexual partners. In other words, just being monogamous within a couple won't make your family relationships less complicated purely on the basis of numbers.

True, the nature of our three-person family is different from that of a monogamous couple with a child, adult or otherwise, but the number of relationships that can add to the strength of our family is the same. The big difference is expectation, and here we feel that our choice to be a family of adults really helps fulfill that original marriage promise. Unlike with children, we don't expect to help each other become better individuals who will then move on; we expect to stay in this family and support it in a direct way for the foreseeable future. We each contribute emotionally, financially, and physically to maintaining the family. In return, we all get support to explore and express the unique strengths that we have to help us deal with our unique limitations. Supporting each other isn't always easy, but we each agree it is necessary, and we are willing to put in the work even if it takes a bit of coaxing from each other from time to time.

We've been a family of three for many years now, but we are open to adding new members. Ideally we'd love two more adults, another woman and another man. That's an ideal, not a necessity, and clearly not a need since we seem to be doing just fine as we are. That goes back to the poem from Kahlil Gibran where we are individuals together because of love. We all love each other in many different ways. Our love flows from ourselves and each other. Our love could easily flow to include others if that should come about. Our family is well supported with three pillars, but it could accommodate more. If those people can follow our rules and believe in our philosophy, the resulting family and individuals could be better. There is no hurry here, no animalistic drive pushing us to expand, only an openness and desire to become the best we can be.

The long haul: Over thirty years in a polyfidelitous triad

Rami Henrich

One afternoon when my son was six, he was playing with a friend in the front yard. It was a beautiful fall day and the boys were doing what many boys do on a beautiful fall day: collecting leaves into huge piles and jumping headlong into them. It's amazing how many piles kids can make and how many hours they can entertain themselves doing that!

My partner, Cindy, and I were a few feet away cleaning out the garage, when my son and his friend, Matt, sauntered into the garage covered with leaves from head to toe. Josh said, "Matt wants to know who is the mama? Who is she?" he said, pointing at Cindy.

I replied, "Well, just tell him that I'm your mom."

My son turned to Matt, "That's my mom," he said, pointing to me. A moment later he returned, "Mom, Matt wants to know who Cindy is."

"Just tell her she is part of our family," I said.

"She's part of our family," he said to Matt as they ran into another crackling pile of leaves.

At age six, that answer sufficed, but as my son got older it became more and more difficult for him to come up with an answer that would not only satisfy others but also himself. At the time, there were no easy answers to these seemingly easy questions, no role models or words to describe Cindy's role in our family configuration.

Before going any further, perhaps it would be useful to explain our family's relationship dynamic. Tom and I are legally married. In fact, we were married twice: once in Bombay, India, in 1976 while living in an ashram, and a second time in a Jewish ceremony in my parents' apartment with a handful of family members in attendance. We have two biological children (a daughter born in 1978 and a son born in 1990). Cindy and I have been partners in a relationship since 1983, and we have lived together since 1992.

Cindy and Tom have a close, supportive relationship that involves more than friendship, in part because they have me in common. They have traveled together, and supported one another when either one of them was in relationship turmoil with me. As a result, there is a closeness between them that differs from other friendships. They do not have an intimate sexual relationship, yet they are closely related. If asked if they are polyamorous, both Tom and Cindy would say that they are in a polyamorous relationship but that they do not identify as polyamorous. This is because they are not in love with two people; each of them loves me, and I am the one who has multiple loves. I deeply love both Tom and Cindy, and feel fortunate to have had so much love in my life.

As for myself, I am not entirely sure of how I identify. It is still an unfolding question and answer for me, but for the purposes of this paper, I will refer to myself as polyamorous. Hearing the word for the first time in the mid-'90s and calling myself a polyamorist felt like a bit of a retrofit; giving myself an established name and identity where once there was none. I didn't have a problem with the word, but it felt a bit like a suit of clothing that didn't yet quite fit or like a wool sweater that caused my skin to itch. Regardless of whether it fit perfectly or not, polyamory does describe a life relationship pattern that is meaningful to me and, I have found, to others.

Loving more than one person is not always a walk in the park. Much of my work, as a psychotherapist, focuses on the challenges facing people in polyamorous relationships. It has been a difficult undertaking for my family to carve its own path in the world, and by bringing forth parts of our story here, I hope to articulate some of the difficulties and joys of living an unconventional lifestyle that is still in the margins of today's mainstream culture. When Cindy, Tom and I decided to live together as a family, we hadn't thought it out, we didn't have a plan or a map, and we didn't know anyone else living like this. We just thought we'd give it a go and try it out, telling ourselves, "How difficult could it be?" Not only were there no role models or advisers, but we hardly had the courage to speak with anyone in our community for fear of how they might react to our lifestyle.

LIFE ON THE MARGINS

Slowly, over time, we found our own way, made our own rules and confided in people who we hoped would embrace our relationship configuration. After thirty years of paving our own way, I am now in a position, as a therapist, to listen, consult and relate to the joys and sorrows of others who are pursuing a polyamorous lifestyle. I now facilitate support groups for people who identify as polyamorous or who are exploring polyamory, offer workshops and presentations, and work therapeutically with polyamorous individuals, couples, triads, quads, etc....Unlike our own haphazard beginnings, I now suggest moving forward slowly and with caution.

Issues of marginalization are an ongoing challenge for people in polyamorous relationships, and our family has had its fair share. I am no stranger to life on the margins: not only do I have two primary relationships, but I am also a woman, Jewish, and over sixty-five. Any one of those identities would suffice as a marginal subgroup, but I believe combining them creates a subgroup of its own. In coming up against societal norms, I have often been fearful of how family, friends and colleagues might react, as well as how people from circles that naturally extend beyond the family such as my children's friends and their families, schools and teachers, and the larger community might behave towards us. Marginalization occurs daily in small and large ways, from inside of the relationship, from extended family members, and from the world, and it has proven to be a difficult and interesting challenge.

Coming Out

Wondering who, if and when to tell people has been one of the biggest challenges facing our family, and in the beginning "coming out" to our immediate family members was the subject of frequent discussions. I feared that my parents, who were quite modern but also quite conservative, would believe that it might be in the best interest of my youngest to remove him from our household and raise him themselves, so I held off from telling them until my son was a teenager and my parents would be too old to pose a threat. Sadly for me, I had underestimated my mother's response, which ended up being loving and accepting, and a bit wistful as well. "I always suspected it," she said. "I am so happy that you have so much love in your life. I can tell that both Cindy and Tom love you, so what could be wrong with that! I only knew your father, and sometimes I wonder if I had it to do over again, well, if I might have been with a woman." That was quite a shocker, and I wished that I'd had the courage to tell her sooner.

My father was another story. He questioned Cindy for seventeen years about why she wasn't married and wondered why she was living with us, but advised by my mother to leave well enough alone, we did just that. My brother, my sister and their partners and children were told early on in the relationship, but to this day we haven't had lengthy discussions about our relationship dynamic. The good news is that everyone accepts it in their own way; the bad news is that it sometimes feels very much like a "don't ask/don't tell" situation in which no one really wants to know more or support the relationship explicitly. Perhaps they believe that it is none of their business, which is fine too.

Role Definition

Another issue that has surfaced time and again over the past thirty years has to do with defining our roles. Who is who, and how do we explain ourselves to others? People have made numerous assumptions and drawn many incorrect conclusions in their efforts to make sense of our relationship configuration. Cindy and I have been asked if we are mother and daughter or sisters, and there were times when people assumed that Cindy was Tom's lover, the children's mother, and even our maid. Yes, maid! In the early '90s, I was on the board of a private school and hosted a fundraising event at my home. Cindy was in the kitchen helping herself to a glass of wine when one of the guests had also gone in the kitchen to get a plate. When the guest returned to the living room, she said, "Do you know that your maid is pouring some wine for herself?" These are painful moments for us all, but they put Cindy in an especially difficult position.

When Tom and I step out into the world, there are no queries about our relationship. Even though I am seven years older than him, it is fairly clear to most people that we are a couple. But when Cindy and I step out into the world, who we are as a couple is less clear and often interpreted as some other type of relationship. When the three of us step out into the world, a whole different scenario unfolds. It is difficult to know what people are thinking, because in our experience, ninety-nine percent of people do not ask about our relationship, either because the possibility of a trio doesn't even enter into their mind or because they suspect but are too embarrassed to ask. For over twenty years now, our family has lived in the same house, on the same block. Neighbors see us come and go, neighbors come over for parties, and neighbors are neighborly, yet not one person has ever inquired about our relationship. On the one hand,

I feel relieved to know that we are at least tolerated, but on the other hand I don't feel known or accepted, and I'm left wondering what people think about us.

The Hushers

In our culture, it is a huge privilege and rank to be in a monogamous heterosexual relationship, and for those of us who exist outside of that cultural norm, it can be difficult if not impossible to avoid internalizing mainstream judgments and criticisms. As a result, over the past three decades, I have lived with an internalized "husher" who conceals my relationship life, and I'm not the only family member who feels this way. In addition to Tom and Cindy having their own hushers to deal with, my children (whose names have been changed in this paper) have also had to live "in the closet" at times. They did not choose this lifestyle; they were not free to say "Sure, go ahead and bring another adult into our life, and let's have you and dad and Cindy as our parents," nor were they free to say "No, we don't want this." The kids did not have a voice in the matter, and I am aware that at times it is an invisible burden that they carry. Not only do we, the adults, have to find ways to describe our relationship, our children have to as well, and like us, they also have to face the possibility of rejection by peers, teachers, the parents of boyfriends or girlfriends, potential spouses, employers, and so on.

Marginalized on the Inside

In addition to the societal marginalization that we experience both internally and externally, marginalization also occurs within the relationship itself. Within a polyamorous relationship, it is very common for one person to feel marginalized by the other two, and this marginalized role is frequently passed around and experienced by each member at one time or another. Sometimes the marginalized role is more frequently occupied by one member of the relationship because of contributing external forces. For example, in our relationship, Cindy does not have the protections that heterosexuality and legal marriage offer me and Tom, nor does she possess the status of being my "first" partner or a biological parent to our children. At other times, Tom is the more marginalized person in the relationship, because, as psychotherapists, Cindy and I share a "vocabulary" and way of looking at life that sometimes excludes Tom. There are also times when I feel marginalized because Tom and Cindy want to do things together without me, or because I feel forced to choose between them. The worst thing about marginalization within the relationship is its potential to lead to painful jealousies, which is a topic that is near and dear to many a discussion about polyamory.

LOVE, FREEDOM, AND SILENCING THE HUSHER

After years and years of dealing with these various types of marginalization, I find that my internalized husher doesn't want to be hushed any longer. I want to share what it is like to live in the margins, and I want to bring forth new ways of thinking about relationships and families. I want to express the freedoms, and joys, and possibilities that nonconventional relationships can offer. For instance, in our polyamorous relationship, there are the everyday things like sharing the burdens of household chores, parenting with more than two adults, helping each other to process emotional upsets, getting our needs met by more than one person, and the general camaraderie that ensues. If we are planning a party and the three of us are humming along, working as a team, it is so enjoyable and so much more fun!

And then there is the love! The love in this family is far beyond anything I could have imagined. To be deeply loved, appreciated, tolerated, accepted and admired by more than one person is such a privilege and really quite amazing. It is a love that is not limited, a love that expands our abilities to give, to receive and to work on ourselves. Whoo-hoo for that! And, in spite of the many difficulties that our family has faced, I firmly believe that the challenges have also been gifts to us. By following a path of heart, Cindy, Tom, my children and I have all had to learn how to take chances and risks in the face of a disapproving culture. We have put love first, even when it felt dangerous to do so. Is it risky? Yes, I think so, but we have been willing to take the risk, and now I am risking a bit more by sharing our life publicly in this paper. My fingers are crossed as I venture out and ask the question, "Will we be safe?" Guess I will see.

While our family still struggles with when and where to "come out" publicly, there is another more personal part of the polyamorous lifestyle that does not tolerate hiding. In order for a polyamorous relationship to work successfully, each person must be committed to working on themselves. Many monogamous relationships can ignore nagging feelings of jealousy, insecurity, lack of boundaries, etc., because the construct of monogamy, an accepted social structure that provides a measure of safety and security, inherently puts these concerns at ease (at least for some). In a monogamous model of partnership, it is generally clear which relationships and behaviors are legit and which are not. Polyamory offers no such net to fall back on, so jealousies, insecurities, boundaries and the like all have to be explicitly and continually worked on (both personally and in the relationship). Polyamory offers a certain level of personal and relationship freedom that I adore and cherish, and this paper is written in part to present the possibility of creating relationships differently, of stepping outside of the norm, of living life closer to oneself, and allowing the process to unfold. But with that freedom comes the hard work of forging your own way and facing your limits and edges. You must discover who you really are and expand as a person, which is a beautiful and challenging thing to do.

Recently a colleague who attended one of my presentations said, "What I am taking away from this presentation about polyamory is: double your pleasure and double your pain." There is some truth to this statement. Polyamory blazes a path of personal growth, love, and freedom that can be unbelievably rewarding and unbelievably difficult. It may not be for everybody, but I feel endlessly grateful to have found partners willing to carve out this path with me. I feel a bit shy to say this, but I am so proud of us for having the courage to embark on this journey and for having done the work necessary to sustain it all of these years. In fact, I am proud of everyone who has the courage to follow their own path of heart, however that may look, and this work is in part a testament to them.

Full circle

Elisabeth Sheff

In many other places I have described my disastrous attempt at polyamory and some of the outcomes my family and I experienced.[1] For this book, a shortish summary will give the important background that makes the second half of this story make sense.

THAT WAS THEN

My junior year in college at "Granola U" in northern California, I unexpectedly found myself in love with Rick,[2] a man who had told me (on our first date, no less!) that he never wanted to be monogamous or get married. For the next ten years I dragged my feet, with him trying to talk me into finding us a girlfriend (long before we had heard the term unicorn) and me trying to manipulate agreements so that he felt like he could be potentially non-monogamous but I would not have to deal with him actually being

---

1   The most detailed discussion is in chapter four of my book *The Polyamorists Next Door: Inside Multiple-Partner Relationships and Families* (2014, Rowman and Littlefield). The best audio version is the interview I did in 2010 with Cunning Minx and Ken Haslam at *Polyamory Weekly*, "Poly Families: New Sociological Research," *polyweekly.com/?s=sociology+of+poly+families*

2   All names except my own are pseudonyms.

non-monogamous.[3] Increasingly frustrated with the seem-ingly endless negotiation and tired of tottering perpetually on the verge of becoming polyamorous, in 2002 I finally felt like I had reached a crossroads. Deciding to finally take the plunge and stop the manipulative stalling, I told Rick I was never going to find us a unicorn and that if he wanted one he should go out and get himself a girlfriend, no holds barred. What is most important in this story is that, at the crucial decision point where it was up to me to pursue polyamory or not, I decided we had to try or we would never be able to finally put the issue to rest. I was afraid that, after such a long and tedious approach, if we shied away at the last second then the cloud of indecision would haunt us forever. Turns out, trying polyamory out of fear is not such a good idea.

Rick's experiences with dating were less than satis-fying. He dated Dylan, a mutual friend, and their relation-ship did not work out. Dylan and I had been close before, and in a chain of events I still don't quite understand, her falling out with Rick soured our friendship as well. Dylan had been dear to me, and I missed her and her son. While Rick became increasingly disillusioned with his search for a real connection, I simultaneously fell in love with Steve. Neither Rick nor I had anticipated that I would fall in love with a man, because I am a lesbian-leaning bisexual and both of us had expected a woman. Dismayed by the dearth of girlfriends and alarmed at my growing connection with Steve, Rick asked me to be monogamous and marry him.

---

3   Rick could date any woman he would like, as long as 1) she was OK with me and the kids, and 2) she was from Mars.

I was irate, furious that he would refuse marriage when I had asked him years before, but willing to marry now that someone else wanted me. Even worse, he had repeatedly assured me that he was seeking an expanded family, not just sex with multiple women. The moment it looked like we might form that family with a man, not a woman, Rick could not handle it and wanted to become monogamous.

Even though I got what I had initially wanted—marriage and monogamy—it was not the way I wanted it to be. I felt betrayed and enraged, wanting to leave with every fiber of my being, but wanting to stay so my small children could have their parents together. For five of the longest years of my life I tried everything I could think of to move past what I came to think of as "the poly debacle" and become happier and more content in my relationship. When I realized that the relationship between me and Rick had plateaued in healing and was not going to get any better, it hit me full force that I had to get a divorce or become a bitter and angry disaster. After fifteen years together and two years of legal marriage, it was time for Rick and me to go our separate ways—sort of. We still had two young children to whom both of us were (and remain) completely devoted.

Co-parenting with Rick after the romantic portion of our relationship ended meant ongoing contact—in person, on the phone, email, and texting to decide where the children would be, when, and who would take care of them. Ending our romantic relationship also did not mean an end to our previous conflicts, which continued right along, though sometimes in new and different forms. We no longer fought about how to structure our romantic lives, instead we fought more about the kids and sometimes money. As we got better at being exes, our co-parenting became smoother and we could comfortably interact at birthday parties and school events. Issues and conflicts still arose, but they became easier to deal with on the whole and less tinged by past betrayals as the years passed.

THIS IS NOW

Nearly fifteen years since I made the decision to encourage Rick to pursue polyamory, I am faced again with the choice of trying polyamory or not. In the intervening time, everything in my life seemed to completely fall apart, and eventually I rebuilt myself. Even though my professional life is in constant flux, I feel surprisingly stable, probably more so than at any other point in my life. Things are pretty good with Rick and me, and though we still occasionally fight about the kids and money, we are mostly on the same page and friendly the vast majority of the time. The children are in good shape, leading intensely average lives among peers who have a variety of parental configurations. While our kids have undoubtedly been affected by the divorce, Rick and I get along far better than some of the other families we know, so our kids see a far more congenial and collaborative family life than they witness among some of their peers.

My romantic life has moved ahead as well. For the past three years I have been with Kira, a smart and feisty woman who makes me smile. Planning to marry in the fall of 2015, we await the US Supreme Court decision regarding same-sex marriage at the national level as this book goes to press. Kira and I are in a happily monoga-mish relationship that we have rarely expanded to include joint or individual trysts with others. Constantly working (academicians are never done with their work; there is always something else to read, write, or grade) and trying to make time to see each other while we manage our busy lives, neither Kira nor I is eager to go out searching for flings. Our monogamish agreement is fluid and mostly focused on honesty, with each of us considering how we feel as things go along and discussing it to explore our boundaries. Because Kira's sex drive is higher than mine, we had both thought it would be her testing the bound-aries more often.

It seems like things never go as expected when it comes to polyamory. Recently, someone came along who is just my type—adorable, playful, earnest, smart, open-minded, conversational—"Jackie" is everything I find appealing in a partner. Jackie is also living in a poly triad with my dear friends W and Q, who introduced me to Jackie and fully endorse my connection with her. Kira has encouraged me to hang out with Jackie and is fine with me having a fling with Jackie. What does not work for Kira is ongoing socializing in which Jackie and I engage in public displays of affection in front of Kira. Some poly families can deal with that, but it is a common hard line for folks new to non-monogamy, who might be ok with their partner having other partners, but not right in front of them. For other people, right in front of them is the only way they can feel comfortable, by keeping the (usually couple) relation-ship as a package deal for any outsiders wishing to play.

For Kira, the optimum monogamish relationship

would be occasional flings as they present themselves, but pretty much monogamous most of the time. I, on the other hand, have a more communal approach in general—I am usually the one to invite people over or encourage people to join in spontaneously in a way that Kira sometimes finds intrusive. Over the years with Kira, I have consciously tempered my knee-jerk communalism. Still, my more-the-merrier attitude comes out in many ways—I am polyfoodious[4] and polyaffective, in that I value some friendships like family and have long-term, emotionally intimate relationships with a small number of people, most of whom have not been my lovers. Friendship has always been very important to me,[5] and I have always been able to get many of my emotional needs met through friendship. While I enjoy sex, it is not that big of a deal to me,[6] and most of my partners have had higher sex drives than mine.

During the process of writing this book I happen to find myself again at the crossroads—do I pursue something with Jackie that promises to be potentially erotically and emotionally satisfying, even if my wife (to be) feels

---

4   Polyfoodious is a word I made up just now to describe my feeling that other people's food is always better and I want to eat their food. Even if I have the same thing, theirs must be better. I am happy to share my own food as well, but it takes a great strength of will on my part to refrain from attacking your dessert. May I have a bite?

5   A trait that is one of the many reasons I am eternally grateful to my dear mother.

6   Ironically, sex is not that personally important to me, given that I am a "sex researcher," even though I would be viewed as a family researcher if the families I studied were monogamous.

uncomfortable with a potential ongoing secondary-esque connection between me and Jackie? Given the degree of satisfaction I get from my friendship with Jackie and the fun we have just hanging out, and the fact that Kira is fine with me being friends with Jackie and feels no need to put any limitations on that relationship, I think I am going to stick with polyaffective relationships in this case, rather than polyamorous ones. As I said, Jackie is just my type, and I could see falling for her in a big way. By keeping our relationship at the level of a non-sexual friendship[7] I can enjoy hanging out with her and still avoid upsetting my home life. Having come full circle, I am making a different choice this time. Things are too good and I have way too much to lose to risk it again.

GLEANINGS FROM THE POLY FOLKS

Initially I had titled this section "Teachings from the poly folks," but it sounded too intentional. It is not as if the poly people I met and interviewed, hung out with and got to know had intentionally taught me about relationships. In fact, I have learned as much from how some relationships did not work out at all as I have from happy/functional/healthy relationships. Instead, it often feels as if I have followed this wandering tribe and sifted through the bits they left behind—gleaning what I could from their words, thoughts and artifacts.

One of the main things I have learned is that each relationship is its own self, an idiosyncratic thing/event/process that should be accorded its own merit (or lack

---

7   Friends without benefits?

thereof). Relationships do not have to continue simply because they existed at one point, and making rules about how people will feel does not actually translate to determining how people will feel in reality.

Through a process of coming to know myself and what I want out of a relationship, I have decided internally not to pursue a potentially problematic relationship. It is a choice I could not have made in my relationship with Rick because there was so much coercion leading up to it and so much intensity riding on the relationship with Steve that I could barely stay with Rick after he asked me to marry him only in response to Steve's desire for me. Things are very, very different with Kira because I don't have to constantly protect myself from her, I can relax and simply be who I am without fending off constant pressure. As I got to know Kira better, my waning wariness was disconcerting at first, like a familiar toothache finally gone that leaves an empty space in the gums that the tongue just has to explore occasionally to see if it is really gone. I missed it like that, oddly and fleetingly, before settling into a true match. I recognize how valuable my connection with Kira is and how hard that is to find, especially for me because I do not seem to be attracted to that many people.

I find it ironic that, with so many years studying polyamory and so many dear friends who sustain lovely polyamorous relationships, I decide this time to forgo the poly relationship in order to protect my monogamish marriage. That is a very couple-focused, non-poly decision. Again ironically, it is simultaneously a very poly decision to refrain from sexual involvement with specific people. Poly people do not automatically sleep with everyone they meet—best friends, siblings, and special exes are frequently off limits due to the weirdness it could provoke. Ultimately I take my gleanings from the poly community and relish my friendship with Jackie, as well as my co-parenting relationship with Rick. Free to construct relationships as I see fit, I decide to prioritize my relationship with Kira precisely because she freely allows me to have a friendship with Jackie. To Jackie's credit, she is willing to have a close friendship that does not involve sex but still provides us both with emotionally intimate and mutually supportive companionship. That level of affection and willingness to continue contact, outside of the potential for sexuality, is the root of not only polyamorous and polyaffective relationships, but enduring relationships in general. That is the best poly gleaning of them all.

On leaving without saying goodbye

Andrea Zanin

He and I met in 2007. It was Toronto Pride, so I was visiting from Montreal, and we were set up by friends at a dinner party—unbeknownst to me, but knownst to him. I don't believe in love at first sight, but love at first sight didn't care, and happened anyway. Like a punch in the stomach, the sight of him winded me. I had to catch my breath and greet eight or ten other people before I could trust myself to say hello to such a beautiful creature as he.

We talked all night. He left without saying goodbye, which I found puzzling, but I wasn't deterred. I got his e-mail address. He told our friends he liked me. We flirted the next day at the Pride parade, him on stilts in tiny leather shorts, me on foot with a Leather pride flag, both of us sweaty in the blistering heat. A whirlwind courtship ensued—I pursued him, he responded. We had a disastrous first date in Ottawa. He was on crutches thanks to recent knee surgery, my leg was hurting persistently for no good reason, and we were both too broke to pay for a hotel, so we consummated our love in my parents' basement while they were out of town, like teenagers sneaking about. Six weeks later he was wearing my collar and we were apartment-hunting. I moved to Toronto on New Year's

Day, with snowdrifts filling the truck as we packed.

We were both poly and kinky before we met. I think we were both relieved not to be each other's first. (What's that Starhawk poem? "I bless those who have taught you and those who have pleased you and those who have hurt you. / All those who have made you who you are.") We commissioned a custom stainless steel chain, no clasp, and I placed it around his neck, fastened the links together with pliers. He finished his master's degree and got a job. The recession hit and we acquired a roommate for a month, which turned into six years. I met someone else a few months in, and soon we were a triad. That came to an end two and a half years later. He hooked up with an old friend, and soon we were in another triad. The three of us appeared on TV. They filmed us as we did our scheduling, armed with coloured highlighters and well-honed communication skills.

Nobody could quite figure out what was wrong with my leg. I started and finished my master's, then started a PhD. I was diagnosed with spinal cord cancer. Recovery from surgery didn't go as planned. Chronic pain became a full-time partner. His scoliosis and migraines worsened. Our partner herniated a couple of discs and had surgery for thyroid cancer. The triad became a support structure for our health care obligations. We joked about buying shares in the back clinic; the receptionists sent us Christmas cards. We squeezed as much joy out of life as we possibly could.

He hooked up with a younger guy. The two of us, his new guy and our roommate moved into a house a block away from our partner. We called our place the South Wing, and hers the North Wing. We shared a vehicle, vacation plans, video games. So much pain, so many pills and procedures. We were so tired. Things became increasingly fragile. I met someone new. Not a punch in the stomach, no, more like... a musical note I hadn't heard in a very long time, a song I began to softly hum all the time, a reminder of something I'd forgotten. The triad came to a close after three and a half years. Our household was no longer the South Wing, became just a house with four people trying their best. New love grew against all odds, bending time and space to carve out its existence. A divorce. Child custody arrangements. Long hours on the phone. There was another moving van on the highway from Montreal on another cold day, an apartment up the street. I met her kids and we were shy with each other.

After our triad broke up, he and I couldn't seem to find our footing. So much change, so much pain, so much love, so much processing. A year later, we wrote a contract, for the first time in our relationship, trying to hammer out all the things we would each do to get back what we'd lost—or rather, we said, to move forward into something new. Somehow, the writing of it made things clear to me, showed me that we were putting our effort into the wrong place. It was time to work on being something else to each other instead. So I left. I moved up the street, past the old North Wing, and into the apartment my partner and I had found for her a year before. Now it would be home to us both. She had licked her wounds there when her life changed to make room for me. My turn to do the same. There's sadness between these walls, right now, but also so much music. Sometimes I watch her sleep and it is like looking at an angel. We have so many dreams.

A month ago, I walked down the street. We shared a meal and then I removed his collar. The pliers blurred as I worked to break the links that had held fast for seven years, and he soaked my skirt with tears. We held each other close in the room that had once been ours. I split some more links, and we each kept half the chain. I don't know what that symbolizes, yet.

We are so focused, as marginalized people, on creating and building a new thing, with no role models and few useful paradigms. Even defending our right to do this creative work is itself an occupation that requires real time investment. As ever, those who deviate from the norm are asked to endlessly explain why, while the norm itself evades question and study. And then there's the sheer time management, the emotional energy and logistical density, of the thing itself, this thing we are so focused on creating. Doing a new thing is never easy. There are no blueprints, no recipes. We must bake from scratch.

And all of this means that we don't often think about endings. About the process of dissolving the structures we have so carefully laboured to construct. All our pains-taking effort isn't for naught; for something to end means it had to have existed, and the existing is what counts. It's just that in the same ways as our building is complex, so is our dismantling. I get why convention is so appealing. In some ways it might mean we'd get more time to rest. For me, and for many of us, convention is too tight a space for us to really live in, but its blueprints are everywhere. Sometimes I glance at them.

To me, poly family is a means, not an end. An approach

to the world, an idea, but not a blueprint. I'm not sure I trust blueprints, anyway. They stay static while reality persistently changes all around them. As poly people, our relationships are no more and no less stable, lasting or happy than any others; but those three elements do not always occur, together or separately, even in the most conventional of arrangements. We just make different choices about process, about how we want things to work, not necessarily where we want them to end up. We start building a structure, we add on a room, we change the plan to accommodate what happens. Three baths and an unfinished basement. We make it work as best we can, same as anyone else. We double a recipe, make it gluten-free and substitute applesauce for eggs. We call it something new and we feed each other.

So here I am, a queer poly poster child of sorts, sitting in my comfy chair in the apartment I now share with my partner—my only partner. Up the street from the home I shared, until recently, with my partner of seven-plus years, his young partner of two, and our roommate of six. Around the block from a person he and I had hoped to be with for many years. (Sometimes I run into her at the grocery store. She's dating someone sweet these days. We hug by the Ontario apples and ask about each other's lives.) I'm writing about endings, but I'm not sure I know anything wise about them. I do know that we must adapt to an empty room with as much creativity as we built it in the first place.

How do we grieve? I don't know. I'm figuring it out. For me, so far, it looks like having brunch every three weeks with this person whom I, for seven years, had expected to grow old with. Removing his name from my health insurance, but only after he gets some dental work and refills his migraine prescription, because I want him to be okay. Texting him to ask him to leave the hand mixer on the porch because I forgot it when I moved. Now I need it to bake cupcakes for a five-year-old's birthday party.

Poly family looks like making drives to Montreal, also about every three weeks, to stay with leather family and spend time with my partner's two kids, whom I've discovered I love quite fiercely. I never wanted to have any children of my own, so this works out nicely: I didn't have them—they showed up already had. There are no right words quite yet for this quasi-parental experience. Sometimes I wish he could have been a part of it.

Poly family looks like wanting to grow old with someone new, and not knowing who else might join us—together or individually—along the way. Grief looks like crying while I write this piece, and smiling too, and wishing it could have been different, and knowing that we did our best, and that each of us is doing our best right now. No blueprints for this part either.

Poly family means being neighbours, and sometimes friends, perhaps friends who carry a small piece of chain with them and have no words for it. Poly family means trusting my leatherfolk to come through, because romantic partners and metamours have never been the only people who count as family around here. It means refusing the narrative that says endings must mean never speaking to each other again, that love must die instead of changing shapes. Sometimes it means drawing boundaries, yes. But it also means we can leave without saying goodbye.

Part VI: Racy bits

The varying beauty of leather relationships

Phyllis-Serene Rawley

My former husband and his new submissive and I were hanging around one weekend and I thought the coincidence of this pic would make a good topic for examination. Sooooo…while they were off in the bedroom getting their kink on, I wrote this piece about the unique qualities of being in a dual bi, kinky, double Dom, swinger positive, poly and open marriage…

I realize that alone could stop all other conversations at the Thanksgiving dinner table and it should. But dear kinkster, realize we didn't all wake up one day and decide we were kinky or bi or poly. We took our time and with each subsequent orgasm, when our creative juices flowed over us like Niagara Falls, we thought about ever-increasing ways to increase our pleasure. And when pleasure is shared it has a wonderful bonding effect that, in our case, made our marriage of ten years work.

My husband and I met as kinksters, so we were halfway to home base. We each had our own paths that brought us together. But the basis for the marriage was open communication, exploration, and a sense that life is about the journey, not destiny.

Don't get me wrong—the first few years of marriage we shared our home with the green monster of jealousy. But somewhere between living together, knowing each other, fighting the enemies within as well as without (illness, job loss, community gossip, jealous subs, etc.), we found within each other a strong support to lean on.

My response to the question of jealousy has been, "I have his heart and his wallet. His dick can go anywhere." Why? Because he and I both get to come home to love and acceptance. And that's still very hard to find out there anywhere, vanilla or kink, swing or poly.

Man has proven it is not a species that mates for life, though the constructs of our community, primarily through religious institutions, develop marriage as a contract that allows for social control. Marriages are hard-pressed to survive under any pressure, let alone thrive year after year. The marriages that make it for any length of time do so because they share something of value. It could be the love, the kids, the money, the sex or the comfort. If you are lucky you learn that the value you share is the love for each other. I was able to say goodbye to jealousy once and for all when I faced all the fears it brought up, discussed them, and then went forward trusting (and testing) the marriage commitment.

I came to marriage not because I needed a man, but because I wanted one. I wanted to share the journey. I suspected my life would be fuller with someone I could tell my wild stories to, eat popcorn and ice cream for dinner with, and lust after the same hot bodies over. What a dream come true, I was one lucky fucking bitch! And I enjoyed it, while it lasted.

The influence of polyamory on sexuality

Wilrieke Sophia

It seems that polyamory is firmly connected with the belief of having sex with multiple partners. Very often the prejudice goes that the reason for being polyamorous is the freedom to be sexually active in a liberal way. You're polyamorous? You must be into sex big time.

THE CONNECTION BETWEEN POLYAMORY AND SEX

I'm living in a polyamorous way for a while now. Was the reason for me to open up my relationship primarily based on my sexual desires?

I have to disappoint you here. It wasn't.

Didn't it even play a small role? It did. My partner and I were a bit disappointed that now we've found each other, we were expected to never kiss, cuddle or make love with another person for the rest of our entire lives. We both didn't have that much experience with others, and speaking for myself, most of the experience I did have wasn't so nice at all. Yes, I was curious about having sex with others and the thought of being able to freely feel this desire made and makes me very happy. I know that I have the full freedom to explore what I want to experience and find the right people to create memories with.

The main reason for me to open up my relationship, though, was for reasons of self-growth.

SEX AS A PERSONAL GROWTH EXPERIENCE

My life is based on personal growth. Getting to know myself better, stretching the borders of my comfort zone, creating a life that is becoming more and more amazing day by day is what really turns me on. Being afraid or insecure is not something I try to avoid. It's more of the opposite: being scared or insecure means that there is a lesson to be learned. A belief to let go of. An inner child to be hugged.

I love to find out which actions can help me grow. For example, when I realized that I was very insecure about my body, I started to go dancing on my own and try to see myself through the eyes of others. I noticed that when I was feeling shy, the people liked me. I noticed that when I was feeling open, the people liked me. I noticed that when I told the people I liked honestly that I thought they were amazing, they responded to me that they thought I was awesome. I learned to like me and to appreciate the package given to me.

When I became aware that I was afraid of letting people come close both physically *and* emotionally (one of both is easier), I started to hug my friends. I learned that I could touch the people I loved without being afraid of being hurt.

In the same way, sex can be an amazing personal growth opportunity. When you have trouble letting go of control, D/s play could be a helpful (and pleasant) way to learn to let go of control in a safe way. But what if D/s really attracts you and your partner is insecure about his sexuality or not into D/s? Finding another compatible partner to explore your sexuality with can be a transformative experience for your inner processes.

Are you spiritual and very much into feeling energies? Tantra is an amazing way of physically connecting. Tantra includes much more than sex, by the way. What if your partner is more the physical-kinda-bouncer and not into the *zweverige*[i] stuff? Should you just forget about it?

BRINGING NEW EXPERIENCES INTO YOUR EXISTING RELATIONSHIP

Long-term relationships are known for becoming boring. Especially inside the bedroom. Year in, year out the same routine of positions and actions without much new. Maybe you are an adventurous couple and you've tried some toys, but what I hear from a lot of people is that they miss the arousal they felt when they were in love.

Polyamory gives you the opportunity to fall in love with other people and be intimate with them. You know what increases your desire for having sex? Having sex! Can you imagine what happens with your existing relationship when you fall in love with someone else and have sex with this person? You will go back home, full of lust-hormones, butterflies in your stomach and never-ending energy, and jump your partner. You will. ☺

Besides the new energy you put into your existing

---

1   Dutch, *floating.*

relationship, you will also gain new experiences and bring them back home. You might discover new techniques, positions or whole new ways to approach sex with other people. Bringing these things back into your existing relationship can really spice things up for both of you.

ABUNDANT SEX IS SEXY

What is the most scary thing I can imagine? Giving my partner his freedom. I can hold him close by reinforcing the conditioning that he has to be faithful to me by not having physical connections with others. I could even marry him as a sign that he is now "my husband." My property. It's a relationship based on fear.

When I let go of the fear-based boundaries of our relationship and give him the freedom to explore whatever connection he builds with another woman, there is no need for him to stay with me because "he should." The only reason for him to stay with me is because *he really wants to be with me.*

I have the liberty to connect with other people whenever and how I like. That means I don't have to stay with him for reasons based on scarcity. "If I want sex, I need him to be willing to have sex with me" becomes "If I want sex I could just find someone who's willing to have sex with me." Considering the population density in the Netherlands, that shouldn't be a tough job. Instead, I'll have sex with my partner because I want to have sex with *my partner.* I freely choose to spend time and have sex with my partner and not because I'm not allowed to fulfill my desires anywhere else. Can you imagine anything more sexy than a person who totally freely chooses to be with you? It makes me feel very special and desired.

DO I RECOMMEND USING POLYAMORY TO SPICE UP YOUR SEX LIFE?

A polyamorous relationship boosts your sexuality. You will learn new things and bring renewed energy into your existing relationship. Would I recommend opening up your relationship in order to give your sex life a boost?

No.

Please, never let sex be the main reason for a polyamorous relationship. If you want to have sex with others, try swinging together. Swinging is having sex with others without further commitment, usually practiced as a couple.

Polyamory is so much more than having sex with multiple partners. When your partner is with someone else, you are very likely to be challenged by being afraid he likes that other person more than he likes you, he will leave you, he doesn't like you, feelings of jealousy, sadness and much more. You have to be willing to face into the mirror that is held up for you, and realize these feelings come from within you. He does love you, but you don't love yourself enough to understand it. He doesn't like her better than you. She can teach him different things. It's not a race of who is the best. The different connections are just different, bringing different things.

When you are willing to dive deep into your fears and insecurities, you will learn to let them go. It will help you to become more *you*, more centered, loving, fearless and happy.

Polyamory is much more than being a sexual person. To me, polyamory is part of a lifestyle of personal growth. A path of love, letting go, being in the moment and enjoying life to the fullest. And *that's* what makes my sexuality blossom.

Erotic vignettes

Robert Beveridge

CRYSTALLINE

There are three sides
to every triangle, and most
are unequal. Constant vigilance
keeps angles sharp, fresh,
trims extraneous branches
from the trunk. It is impossible
when one drops seed into furrow
to predict the kind of fruit
it will bear, yet still we
keep shears handy, water
saplings with tears, rust,
deep exploratory kisses in the rain.

Each leaf is a celebration,
a potential, an opportunity
for front-porch quarterbacks.
The pool's kitty mounts,
two to one on starfruit,
quince an outsider at twelve.
No one ever lays two bucks
on the humble beechnut.

Hands join, lips raise
in supplication. Another
harvest is begun.

SHARED

The scourge of the internet: duckface.
You see it everywhere, in selfies,
on politicians, burned onto toast
in the manner of miracles. I give thanks
every day you never developed the habit,
selfie-loving wife. The look in your
pictures is earnest, forthright, clear
eyes, lips curled in that private
wicked smile that seduces. The other,
after, was our secret. You call it
your melted-butter smile, when after
love you are so satisfied your bones
have turned to margarine, your brain
to jelly.
       I got home last Sunday,
found you naked, sprawled atop
the sheets. You and your lover
had been so eager you didn't stop
to pull them down. I stripped,
slipped in behind you, asked if you'd
had a good time. When I kissed
you, my tongue turned to toast.

A CLOUDED VIEW

The difference between the knowledge
of the piston's action and the sight

of piston as it sinks into cylinder.
The blood that pulses faster, the fire
stoked deep within electric sparkplug
crackle.

Branches twist, intertwine
in the wind, tongue meets tongue
as lovers kiss in the backseat beneath
the largest tree in the wood.

You know
you are watched, moan louder in response.
Lips twitch, thighs shift. His tongue
traces your pendant, heart shot through
with infinity symbol or, perhaps,
Moebius strip. The eyes excite
you, make every thrust feel harder. His
fingers on your hips guide you to hands,
knees, and you feel him slip into you again
inch after lovely inch. You loop up, meet
the eyes of the half-concealed voyeur
who takes his own pleasure, and smile.

THE LAST TURN

You've been there. The directions
are perfect until the penultimate
boulevard, then your friend says
"you'll go about two and a half
miles until you see the unlabeled
turn just past Jackson's Oak
which isn't there anymore but you
will see where it was, and the turn
is choked with weeds and doesn't

look like a serviceable trail
but a mile and a half later it turns
into Existential Crisis Road."

It's the same as when you get
to *those* three bards in "Pierrot
Lunaire" or the final bag
of frozen raspberries doesn't
fit in the freezer or that
minor infraction from twenty
years ago—say you stole
a pack of baseball cards
and got caught—resurfaces
in your head, taunts you
with the stupidity of it. You hear
Jimmy Sheldon, your best friend
in seventh grade, laugh that you
didn't even get a single Yankee.
Like a desire for bacon when all
you have in the house is cuttlefish
and eight kinds of mustard.

And so you find yourself six
miles later outraced by the local
sloth populace, your eyes stuck
to the shoulder, on a quest
for that patch of weeds just different
enough from every other
to promise you egress.

POLLINATION

How the tallest pistils make
the sweetest honey, but only
given the perfect stigma.
How they combine, become more
than their ingredients, complexity
and texture, perfect admixture
of salty notes, the undertone
of dark sweet nectar. How it slips
off the tongue, slippery, dares
you to catch it with an inhale.
You know you will never drizzle
that stuff from the bear
on your berries, your lips,
your lover's body ever again.

Contributors

ALEXANDER MALCOLM

Alexander is eight years old and loves playing video games. His favorites are Minecraft, Pokémon and Mario. When he grows up, he wants to be a game designer (video games and board games). Though he spent most of his earliest years living in Malaysia with his parents, he now lives with them and his brother in the United States and hopes to stay there for a while.

ANDREA ZANIN

Andrea Zanin writes a lot about sex, relationships and BDSM/leather/kink. She blogs at *sexgeek.wordpress.com*. Andrea is pursuing a PhD in gender, feminist and women's studies at York University with a focus on Canadian leatherdyke history. She has been teaching about queer sexuality, non-monogamy and BDSM/leather internationally for over a decade, and she endeavors to bring an awareness of privilege and oppression to all her work. She lives in Toronto and enjoys eating fine dark chocolate and wearing really nice shoes. Find her on Twitter at @sexgeekAZ.

ANGELA CALLAIS

Angela Callais is a queer mama of one, wife, girlfriend and lover of many—in and out of the bedroom. Doula, educator, musician and sex therapist are on the path of the labyrinth that life is taking her on. Intuitive, passionate and nurturing when it comes to sex and relationships, she enjoys pushing boundaries of her own and others. On the flip side, you can often find her bargain shopping for sparkly makeup, dresses and luxury kitchen gadgets.

ANN

Ann is a mad scientist with the best of intentions, and a lover of living and growing things.

DR. ANYA

Dr. Anya is a spiritual counselor and author of *Opening Love: Intentional Relationships & the Evolution of Consciousness* (Changemakers Books). Learn more at *dranya.net*.

AOIFE LEE

Aoife Lee is an equestrian, book nerd, history buff, therapist, rennie-by-marriage, tea enthusiast and social justice advocate. A licensed psychologist, she feels privileged to maintain a practice that serves her community, with a particular emphasis on sexual, relational and gender diversity including affectional identity, BDSM, kink, transgender, polyamory, and other non-monogamies. She is also a part-time professor of psychology and an advocate through her state professional association. Aoife Lee is a pseudonym.

ATHENA AFFAN

Athena Affan is forty, and labels herself as a poly, bi, black woman living on the unceded traditional territories of the Coast Salish people (also known as Vancouver, BC, Canada). She shares her home with two lovely men, a lovely cat and their lovely seventeen-month-old son. Yes, you could say that her life is full of love, and she's so grateful for the opportunity to share that with her readers.

BALDWIN OMNI

At ninteen, Baldwin Omni encountered a couple in an open marriage who opened his eyes. At twenty-two, a friend took him to swinging parties. At twenty-four, he married a woman who wanted an open marriage. Six years later, she changed her mind. Twenty-six years later, she offered him the chance to be poly (not her). Four years later, separation and divorce. Then several attempts at poly relationships. None worked. He met someone mono who just "fits," and he's happy. New path.

CASCADE SPRING COOK AND ZHAHAI SPRING STEWART

Cascade Cook and Zhahai Stewart are relationship coaches living in northern California. Cascade's thesis, *Commitment in Polyamorous Relationships*, Zhahai's writings about New Relationship Energy, and many other poly and relationship resources can be found on their website, *aphroweb.net*.

CHRISTINE AND JAX

Jax lives with his mom, Christine, in Atlanta, Georgia. They enjoy playing Legos and exploring the world together. They live passionately and focus on chasing their happy.

REV. CLAUDIA HALL

Rev. Hall is the community minister of Progressive Faith Church and Ministries. Her ministry is focused on helping people grow spiritually, whatever their religious leanings (or lack thereof). Rev. Hall is a graduate of Saint Paul School of Theology in Kansas City, MO, where she received her MDiv degree. She is a PhD candidate in transdisciplinary studies at the California Institute of Integral Studies. Reach her at *progressivefaithchurch.org*.

DOMINICA MALCOLM

Though born in Australia, Dominica Malcolm lived in Malaysia for five and a half years, before moving to the San Francisco Bay Area in 2014. Her publications include *Adrift*, a novel about a time-travelling pirate; *Amok: An Anthology of Asia-Pacific Speculative Fiction*; and, to be released in 2015, *Marked by Scorn: An Anthology Featuring Non-Traditional Relationships*. Visit her website at *dominica. malcolm.id.au*.

E.

E. knows that if loving you is wrong, she doesn't want to be right.

ELISABETH SHEFF

One of a handful of global experts on polyamory and the foremost international expert on children in polyamorous families, Dr. Elisabeth Sheff is an educational consultant and expert witness serving sexual and gender minorities. She is author of the book *The Polyamorists Next Door: Inside Multiple-Partner Relationships and Families* as well as numerous academic and legal articles pertaining to polyamory, gender, families, and sexual minorities.

JESSICA BURDE

Jessica is a mother, life partner, writer and activist. She is the author of *Polyamory on Purpose*, a blog about the practical side of poly life, and the book *Polyamory and Pregnancy*. She is currently working on her next polyamory-related book, *The Poly Home*. Jessica makes her living as an online marketer supporting local businesses in northeastern Pennsylvania. Since writing "Monosaturated," Jessica has found a wonderful man who is happy to hold her hand while navigating life's challenges.

JULIE FENNELL

Julie Fennell has a PhD in sociology from Brown University and is an associate professor at Gallaudet University. A long-time kinkster and polyamorist, her research currently focuses on the BDSM subculture. She is well known within the subculture as IPCookieMonster, and she blogs about her kinky adventures at *slutphd.com* and is an occasional contributor to *modernpoly.com*.

JULIETTE SIEGFRIED AND MAYA AVERY COMBES

Juliette Siegfried, MPH, is a small-business owner and polyamory activist living in Leiden with her husband Roland of nearly twenty years and his other love Laurel, who is the mother of their six-year old daughter, Maya. Juliette leads a monthly discussion group in Leiden on open relationships.

Maya is the six-year-old daughter of Laurel Avery and Roland Combes. Roland has been married to Juliette Siegfried since 1998 and has been living together with Juliette and Laurel since 2007. They also live with a family friend named Barry, and they all raise Maya together.

KALA PIERSON

Kala Pierson is a composer. In 2015, she was an artist-in-residence or guest composer at the Banff Centre, Tanglewood, the Visby International Centre for Composers, Musikhogskolan Pitea, Wildacres, and the Virginia Center for the Creative Arts. She loves working with choral groups; her most recent commission is to write the mass-choir piece for the 2016 Quadrennial GALA Festival (the world's largest LGBT arts event). Email Kala at *kp@kalapierson.com* or visit *kalapierson.com*.

KATERINA STRATFORD

A professional gypsy in search of the perfect hot wings. I can be bribed to do many things for peanut butter cups. Influences include Anita Blake, Buffy and angry girl music of the indie rock persuasion.

KEVIN GLASS

Kevin Glass is a bioengineering student in the Bay Area. He is interested in refining and designing specialized cells for various applications. Aside from his scientific interests, Kevin also enjoys thinking about the ethical issues surrounding biotechnology and the role that human social structures play in biotechnological development. Kevin also enjoys writing poems and short stories about various aspects of his life, including polyamory and bisexuality.

K.H.

K.H. is a mother, writer, home cook and perpetual reader living in rural Kentucky, where she helps her two partners parent and unschool their four children. She is passionately interested in sustainable living, fermentation, wild foods, yoga and herbal medicine, and will happily talk your ear off on any number of topics. She appreciates old-time music, handmade objects, country living and outside-the-box thinking. She bakes a mean loaf of bread.

KIRSTIN ROHWER

Kirstin Rohwer was born in 1987 and lives in Germany. She currently identifies as a relationship anarchist. One day, when she was annoyed with people confusing some words with each other again and again, she decided to make a little glossary with examples in the form of a comic. It unexpectedly went a bit viral in the online poly world. She hopes it will help people remember the differences between (for example) polygamy and an open relationship.

KITTY CHAMBLISS

Kitty Chambliss authors a blog, *Loving Without Boundaries*, that serves to help create more awareness and acceptance for polyamorous lifestyles and those who practice them, and to let her share knowledge she has gained though her experiences and explorations being polyamorous. She has been with her husband for eleven years, about eight of those years in an open marriage. And she has been with her boyfriend for almost four years now. They are part of a network of close lovers and friends. Kitty Chambliss is a pen name.

LINA

Lina lives together with her wife and their fiancé in a polyfidelitous triad just north of Chicago, Illinois, along with their three cats (maintaining the proper cat-to-person ratio). They work as an office manager, Montessori teacher and cinematographer, respectively. Eventually they hope to add non-furry children to their family. Love and commitment have gotten them this far—though the king-sized bed doesn't hurt—and when they are out to enough people, they will throw a grand party to celebrate that fact.

LOUISA LEONTIADES

Louisa lives in an open relationship with her partners and two children in Sweden. She's the author of *The Husband Swap* and chairwoman of the National Polyamory Association. She also writes for *Huffington Post, Salon, Nerve, Jezebel* and *The Guardian*. She lives a life that makes for a lot of stories.

MARLA RENEE STEWART, MA

Marla Renee Stewart is a professional sex, intimacy and relationship coach and sex educator. Gaining her reputation for being "The Sex Architect," she created Velvet Lips, a sexuality education company, to empower people of all ages to embrace, educate and enjoy their sexuality and their sexual lives. She has studied human sexuality for more than thirteen years at San Francisco State University and Georgia State University. For more detailed information, please go to her personal website: *marlareneestewart.com*.

MAXINE GREEN

Maxine Green is an artist, illustrator and "perfectly sane hatter" by trade, a scientist at heart, and an activist by accident. She contracted activism at the end of 2006, which developed into a full-blown case of event organizing in 2009, when she headed up Polyday in the UK for multiple years, but currently appears to be in remission. She is in ten romantic relationships, nine of which are long distance. Maxine has been known to blog under the name of Emanix, and is also the creator of *chaosbunny.com*.

MELODY

Melody is a proud mom to three extraordinary children. As an active social justice advocate, she believes in love and acceptance and works to eliminate the greed and fear that result from perceived scarcities.

MICHÓN NEAL

Michón Neal writes fantasy romance about unique people in unique circumstances. She is currently working on the Cuil Effect project, a ridiculously long tale about healing, absurdity and all the different ways people interact. Her books are available on Kindle, Smashwords, Scribd, Kobo and more. You can find more details, sneak peeks, links and absurdity on her blog, *Shadow in the Mirror*. Her website is *cuileffect.com*.

NORA

Nora is a mother, a lover, a writer and a lawyer living in Toronto.

PHYLLIS-SERENE RAWLEY

Phyllis Rawley is the visionary founder of Goddess University. Through this leading-edge educational platform, she brings together teachers and healers of all creeds and modalities to share what they've learned. Her goal: to assist our global society to ascend to a higher level of consciousness and heal our planet. Phyllis has an MFA in nonfiction creative writing, a BA in political science and an AS in fashion merchandising. She has sixteen years as a Quaker, twelve years as a missionary and twenty years as a dominatrix.

RAMI HENRICH, L.C.S.W., DIPL. P.W.

Rami Henrich is a licensed clinical social worker, diplomate in process work and sex-positive therapist who works with inner and outer diversity issues and embraces a spectrum of people and their problems. She is co-founder of LifeWorks Psychotherapy Center and the Kink & Poly Aware Chicago Therapists network in Chicago. Rami has studied, taught and applied process-oriented psychology as developed by Arnold Mindell, Ph.D., for over fifteen years. She has a special interest in working with relationship difficulties and those who identify as living an alternative lifestyle.

ROBERT BEVERIDGE

Robert Beveridge is a poet, the driving force behind noise project XTerminal, and allergic to writing short bios. He and his family are currently living in one of Ohio's neoconservative strongholds and planning their escape back to the suburbs of Cleveland as soon as the guards fall asleep.

ROSE MCDONNELL

Rose is a former board member of PolyColumbus, former staff for Beyond the Love, and organizer of Open Hearts Central Ohio. She holds a BA in sociology and psychology. Rose has identified as non- monogamous/polyamorous since she was very young. In addition to her PolyColumbus duties, she has been a mini-summit and registration coordinator for Beyond the Love, has spoken at various polyamory education panels at local universities and made her workshop presentation speaker debut in 2015 at Poly Living in Philadelphia. In real life Rose works at a local library and at the Humanist Community of Central Ohio.

RYAN

Ryan is a socially awkward, introverted, nerdy polymath. His interests include sci-fi (yay Dr Who!), Linux, cosplay, live jamband shows, studying electronics, camping, hockey, festies/conventions, physics thought experiments and taking long walks talking to himself. Today, he is on the verge of getting his associates of applied science in electronics (graduate August 2015), and he does a bi-weekly conversational podcast with his partner Scarlet called *Honest, Open & Vulnerable*. In it, they talk about squee-inducing, awkward, insecure and vulnerable moments; it can be found at *hovpodcast.net.*.

TAMMYJO ECKHART, PHD

TammyJo Eckhart currently lives with her poly, kinky family in Indiana, USA. She is the author of eleven books and has been published in several anthologies and journals. Eckhart is a sought-after book and chocolate reviewer. She is the founder and chief writer for *The Chocolate Cult*. Eckhart holds a PhD in ancient history with minors in women's history and folklore. She is a full-time author but also volunteers for educational and arts programs where she lives. Please check out her website for further information: *tammyjoeckhart.com*.

TIKVA WOLF

Tikva Wolf is the creator of the popular poly webcomic *Kimchi Cuddles*. She's been drawing ever since she could hold a crayon. What she primarily cares about in art (and life) is connecting to people, creating dialogue and spreading awareness. She's always taken delight in making people laugh and unveiling hidden perspectives. She uses humor as a way of being seen deeply, and as a way of encouraging others to deeply see themselves and each other. Contact: *kimchicuddles@gmail.com*; website: *kimchicuddles.com*.

VINY

Figuring out what to say in a bio is Viny's least favorite part of being a writer. Finding out that something she wrote was helpful, or healing, or funny, or inspiring to someone—now that's more like it! Viny's advice column for people in alternative relationships can be found at *dearviny.blogspot.com*.

WILRIEKE SOPHIA

Wilrieke Sophia lives with her partner and three daughters in the Netherlands. They have a non-monogamous relationship. Under the name The Yellow Side of Life, they host cuddle workshops, meetings about non-monogamy and workshops about creating your dream life. Wilrieke is educated in the fields of ecology, tantra, sexuality, personal growth, health, healing, communication, horses and more. She coaches people with or without the assistance of her horses and writes about what inspires her on her blog: *purewilrieke.com.*

ZAC

Zac is forty-four years old, living in Manchester, England, working in the IT industry.

Contributor Index

ALSO FROM THORNTREE PRESS

The Game Changer
A memoir of disruptive love
Franklin Veaux

"A quiet story of trial, error and triumph that fundamentally questions everything we think we know about relationships in general, and polyamory in particular."
— AV Flox

The Husband Swap: A true story of unconventional love
Louisa Leontiades

"Louisa Leontiades has a powerful voice and the courage to live into her questions."
— Lucy H. Pearce, author of *The Rainbow Way* and *Moon Time*

Lessons in Love and Life to My Younger Self: A companion guide to The Husband Swap
Louisa Leontiades with Eve Rickert

"No matter who you are, no matter how you love, there is something here that can make your life better."
— from the foreword by Franklin Veaux, author of *More Than Two* and *The Game Changer*

More Than Two: A practical guide to ethical polyamory

Franklin Veaux and Eve Rickert

"More Than Two may well be the best book on polyamory I've ever read. No joke, it's really that fantastic."

— Andrea Zanin, *Sex Geek*

COMING IN 2016

Ask Me About Polyamory: The Best of Kimchi Cuddles
By Tikva Wolf
With a foreword by Sophie Labelle

Diary of a Rope Slut: An Erotic Memoir
By Emily Bingham
With a foreword by Shay Tiziano

Purple Prose: Bisexuality in Britain
A collection edited by Kate Harrad